MONSTER ARRIVES

"The Thing was upon us in an instant. The monster, black, gigantic. Its chops dripping bloody lather with a sickening noise of mastication, punctuated by the deafening claps of a Titanic colic, lurched down the ravine—beyond us—sweeping rocks aside like pebbles.

"Father Lavagneux and I were petrified. The Indians lay upon their bellies.

"A Keratosaurus! The Keratosaurus of the Arctic Circle alive!" babbled Father Lavagneux as the outrageous Thing stopped and stared at us with disdainful curiosity.

"For 10 long minutes, nailed to the spot, we stared at the prehistoric creature. It stared at us. In full daylight.

"You have seen the Eiffel Tower? In the same manner I have seen the Keratosaurus.

"Its withers stood 25 feet high. Its entire body—from rhinoceros horn to tail tip—must have measured 70 feet. Its hide was like that of the wild boar, covered with two-foot long bristles, gray-black.

"From its hairy belly hung clods of mud as big as a 10-year-old child.

"The noise of its mastication—crackling bones—was like the grinding of ice in a debacle. That of its indigestion was like when a hurricane tears the shrouds out of a big schooner! Its stench overpowered us...

"Then suddenly it raised its head, shook the hills with a long roar and romped down the ravine in gigantic bounds at 40 miles per hour. Its head, held 40 feet above the ground, was the last thing I saw in the whirlwind of rocks hell-racketing behind it!

"THE BEAST HELD IN ITS JAWS WHAT SEEMED TO BE A CARIBOU." –
THE STRAND MAGAZINE (JULY 1908)

COWBOYS & SAURIANS
ICE AGE

By John LeMay

Bicep Books
Roswell, NM

© COPYRIGHT 2020 by John LeMay.

All rights reserved. No portion of the author's original text may be reproduced in any form without permission from the publisher, except as permitted by U.S. copyright law.

First Edition

LeMay, John.
    Cowboys and Saurians: Ice Age
      1. History—Pioneer Era. 2. Cryptozoology
      3. Folklore, Early Twentieth Century.

FOR ALLEN DEBUS, DINOSAUR
WRITER EXTRAORDINAIRE

CONTENTS

INTRODUCTION 9

CHAPTERS
1. THE DUKE AND THE DINOSAUR 15
2. ATTACK OF THE GIANT BEAVERS 65
3. IDAHO BILL AND THE SABERTOOTH TIGER 79
4. PRAIRIE DOG MONSTER OF NEMAHA COUNTY 91
5. BACK TO THE STONE AGE 95
6. SOUTHERN SARKASTODON OF GEORGIA 101
7. MAMMOTHS ALIVE! 109
8. SAGA OF THE SHUNKA WARAK'IN 125
9. PREHISTORIC RHINOCEROS 133
10. THE GIANT SEA COBRA 141
11. MACFARLANE'S BEAR 147
12. A MYSTERY MONSTER 153
13. ICE FISHING WITH A SEA SERPENT 157
14. A HAIRY WATER WHATSIT 169
15. THE DOG EATER 175
16. WHAT WAS THE WAHHOO 193
17. VALLEY OF THE WHISTLING WHATSITS 213
18. SPRING CREEK CAVEMAN 217
19. A HIDEOUS MANEATER 225
20. TYRANNOSAURUS OF THE TUNDRA 231

POSTSCRIPT:
THE REAL LIFE LAND THAT TIME FORGOT 245

ACKNOWLEDGMENTS 255
INDEX 257
ABOUT THE AUTHOR 259

LIST OF ILLUSTRATIONS

1.	THE STRAND ILLUSTRATION	16
2.	PEKING TO PARIS AUTO RACE	19
3.	THE DINOSAURUS!	26/27
4.	RECREATION OF ALLEGED PHOTOGRAPH	35
5.	CERATOSAURUS AND ITS PREY	42
6.	VLADIMIR OBRUCHEV	56
7.	COPE'S DEPICTION OF LAELAPS C.1869	59
8.	GLEESON'S CERATOSAURUS C.1901	61
9.	FUR TRADER, ALBERTA, CANADA C.1880s	67
10.	GIANT BEAVERS BY CHARLES KNIGHT	69
11.	WILLIAM BUDGE	72
12.	SEA SERPENT	78
13.	IDAHO BILL	84
14.	PELT OF AFRICAN MYSTERY CAT	87
15.	SABERTOOTH TIGER	90
16.	GLYPTODON BY ROBERT HORSFALL C.1912	93
17.	ICE AGE MAN	97
18.	PATRIOFELIS BY CHARLES KNIGHT	102
19.	SARKASTODON SKULL C. 1938	104
20.	EARLY DAY MAMMOTH RECONSTRUCTION	110
21.	MAMMOTHS BY CHARLES KNIGHT C.1901	116
22.	RINGDOCUS	124
23.	BAROPHAGUS BY CHARLES KNIGHT C.1902	129
24.	ELASMOTHERIUM BY RASHEVSKY C.1878	132
25.	ELASMOTHERIUM BY CHARLES KNIGHT	135
26.	PRIMITIVE MAN ATTACKING CAVE BEAR	148
27.	CASPAR WHITNEY	150
28.	GRIZZLY ADAMS	151
29.	SIVATHERIUM RESTORATION C.1896	156
30.	CHAIN LAKES SERPENT	164
31.	THE "DOG EATER"	187
32.	BORHYAENA BY CHARLES KNIGHT	188
33.	RENO, NEVADA, LATE 1800s	205
34.	PREHISTORIC BOROPHAGUS	209
35.	BLUE MAN OF THE OZARKS	223
36.	NEANDERTHALS BY CHARLES KNIGHT C.1920	224
37.	TYRANNOSAURUS OF THE TUNDRA	230
38.	TYRANNOSAURUS SKULL C.1911	235
39.	TYRANNOSAURUS BY CHARLES KNIGHT	238
40.	DR. W.D. MATTHEW	241
41.	MT. SHISHALDIN	249
42.	THE GARDEN OF EDEN BY THOMAS COLE C.1828	254

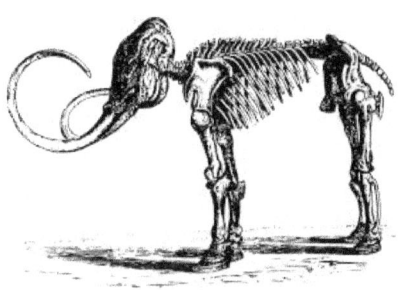

INTRODUCTION:
ICE AGE SURVIVORS

SEQUELS. Ya either love 'em or ya hate 'em. Many times they simply repeat the same formula but with some sort of twist or variation. So, I'll go ahead and just say it: this book is an unabashed repeat of the first...but, as always, with a twist.

Whereas in the first book I explored real reports of remnant dinosaurs printed in pioneer-era newspapers, here I do the same thing, only with the prehistoric survivors of the Ice Age. The last Ice Age, also defined as the Pleistocene Epoch, is estimated to have begun two million years ago and lasted up until about 11,700 years ago. These were, of course, the days of the giant mammoth, saber-toothed tigers, and cavemen. Or, at least, those are the best known examples of Ice Age life in popular culture, but the Ice Age sported a bevy of unique megafauna (or giant animal life) from giant sloths to giant beavers.

To me, a dinosaur-loving kid who thought of everything in terms of movies, the Ice Age was the "sequel" to the age of the dinosaurs. It had a different look and "new monsters." Instead of scaly reptiles in a tropical climate, we had hairy, giant mammals roaming a frozen wasteland. And though the "monsters" of the Ice Age were nowhere near as "cool" as the dinosaurs, they were still undeniably interesting to me.

In fact, the megafauna of the Ice Age naturally had a better chance of survival into the modern era than the dinosaurs did. However, this also poses a rather interesting conundrum. If that is indeed the case, why then are dinosaurian cryptids seemingly more prominent than those relating to prehistoric mammals?

In my opinion, a dinosaur would stand out more than a furry, heretofore unknown mammal that one might see out in the woods.[1] For instance, an early day pioneer spotting a hairy "what's it" along the trail may simply think it to be an ordinary animal that they were currently unfamiliar with. Strange, certainly, but no big deal—except for when

---

[1] That is unless we are talking about something as magnificently large as a mammoth. I'm thinking more along the lines of spotting something like a Protypotherium, which one might mistake for an odd-looking rabbit at a quick glance.

said animals were violent. Then they garnered some attention. I can't tell you how many articles exist with the simple header of "Strange Animal" that tell of some unknown, often cat-like mammal killing livestock. Some of these mystery felines are today identified by cryptozoologists as misplaced lions and panthers (or, ABCs—Alien Big Cats). But some of the descriptions of yonder defied a misplaced panther or lion and seemed to be describing something else entirely.

But still, no one today goes camping in the Rocky Mountains and reports seeing a wooly mammoth—not anymore at least. In my opinion, there's a good chance that remnant mammoths still roamed the North American continent during the days of early exploration and have since died out. The English explorer David Ingram, for instance, made a note of seeing "hairy elephants" in North America in the 1560s. Ingram's notes are, for the most part, considered accurate and reliable.

In 1807, explorer David Thompson heard tales from Native Americans of similar hairy elephant-like creatures in British Columbia, Canada. One intriguing detail that the natives gave was that the beasts slept while leaning against trees. Four years later in the Rocky Mountains—specifically in the vicinity of Jasper, Alberta—Thompson would find footprints of what he thought to be a mammoth.

"I questioned several Indians, none could positively say they have seen him, but their belief I found firm and not to be shaken," Thompson wrote. "I remarked to them, that such an enormous heavy animal must leave indelible marks of his feet, and his feeding. This they all acknowledged, and that they had never seen any marks of him, and therefore could show me none. All I could say did not shake their belief in his existence."[2]

In another journal entry he wrote:

"Continuing our journey in the afternoon we came on the track of a large animal, the snow about six inches deep on the ice; I measured it; four large toes each of four inches in length to each a short claw; the ball of the foot sunk three inches lower than the toes, the hinder part of the foot did not mark well, the length fourteen inches, by eight inches in breadth, walking from north to south, and having passed about six hours. We were in no humor to follow him; the men and Indians would have it to be a young Mammoth and I held it to be the track of a large old grizzled bear; yet the shortness of the nails, the ball of the foot, and its great size was not that of a bear, otherwise that of a very large, old bear, his claws worn away; this the Indians would not allow."[3]

In summary, Thomson said of his theory that,

"The circumstantial evidence of the existence of this animal is sufficient, but notwithstanding the many months the Hunters have traversed this

---

[2] https://mysteriousuniverse.org/2016/04/19th-century-bigfoot-journals/
[3] Ibid.

ICE AGE

extent of country in all directions, and this Animal having never been seen, there is no direct evidence of its existence, yet when I think of all I have seen and heard, if put on my oath, I could neither assert, nor deny, it's existence; for many hundreds of miles of the Rocky Mountains are yet unknown, and through the defiles by which we pass, distant one hundred and twenty miles from each other, we hasten our march as much as possible."[4]

This is but one of many accounts of remnant mammoths covered in this book. There are plenty more.[5] But, mammoths aside, this book is still called *Cowboys & Saurians*; therefore, I allowed for a few saurian stories to be included under one condition: they had to be set in the snow. Enter what may well be the second most famous pioneer era dinosaur after the Tombstone Pterodactyl: the Ceratosaurus of the Arctic Circle. The great beast was the recipient of not one article, but numerous articles over the course of two decades from 1907 to 1927. Though many today knock the story for the creature's very un-dinosaurian behavior (it was described with movements like a kangaroo, something in vogue at the time but disproven today), if you look at it from the opposite perspective, the beast has some modern attributes:

---

[4] https://mysteriousuniverse.org/2018/01/mysterious-encounters-with-supposedly-extinct-ice-age-monsters/

[5] Benjamin Franklin even asked Lewis and Clark to be on the lookout for living mammoths during their famous expedition.

the dinosaur had hair. That dinosaurs could, in fact, grow hair (and feathers), was not discovered by scientists until long after the Partridge Creek articles. Furthermore, most newspaper hoaxes were one-offs, while the Ceratosaurus was covered for 20 years by a reputable reporter. The pros and cons in these stories bounce back and forth to a maddening extent for truth-seekers. And a truth-seeker should always be objective. Therefore I look at these old stories with a skeptical eye at times. Or, in other words, even though I am a proponent for prehistoric survivors (there are simply too many sightings of them to dismiss), I do my best to propose not only why the stories presented here might be true, but also why they may very well not be true. Unlike today's sightings, the fact of the matter is all the witnesses in these stories are long gone. They can't be interviewed to determine the veracity of their accounts. As it is, all we have to go on are the articles themselves and a few public records that can vouch for the witness's actual existence—if we're lucky. Oft times even that is difficult to dig up.

But, to wrap up my rambling, I hope you enjoy this shameless sequel to the first book, which not only covers monstrous megafauna but a few snowbound saurians as well.

THE AUTHOR

JOHN P. LEMAY
Roswell, New Mexico.
January 2020.

1
THE DUKE AND THE DINOSAUR
THE BEAST OF PARTRIDGE CREEK

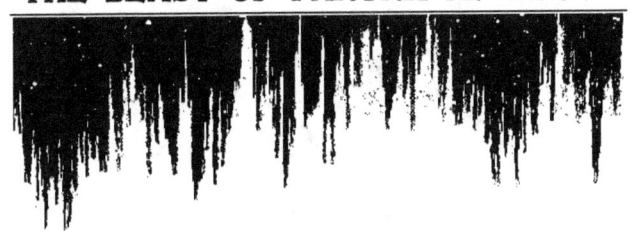

HOPE I DIDN'T GET ANYONE too excited there because this chapter is not about John Wayne blowing away a dinosaur with a 12 gauge. The Duke referred to in the title is the Duke of Westminster, Hugh Grosvenor. The man, an avid hunter and sportsman, made headlines in the early 1900s for traveling to the Yukon Territory to hunt a living dinosaur sighted there. In fact, despite the Tombstone Thunderbird story being one of the best known dinosaur sightings of the Pioneer Period, the story of the Ceratosaurus of the Arctic Circle was better documented. Today it is sadly forgotten by all but a few rabid cryptozoology students.

COWBOYS & SAURIANS

ILLUSTRATION FROM *THE STRAND*.

ICE AGE

The fantastic story began in 1903 and involved the typical Western adventure staples of heading "north to Alaska" for gold prospecting and large game hunting. A banker from San Francisco, James Lewis Buttler, had gone north to Dawson Creek to purchase gold mining concessions. While there, he also wanted to hunt some large game. What he found was much larger than he expected.

Out in the wild, Buttler and his companion, gold prospector Tom Leemore, came across the tracks of a huge monster in the snow. The two men returned to the nearby outpost of Armstrong Creek, where they met with Buttler's friend, George Dupuy, a correspondent for the *Auto*, and Jesuit Priest Pierre Lavagneux. Buttler told the men his tale, and soon after, he returned to the wild to hunt the monster with his two new companions, plus a few members of the Klay-akuk tribe.

As luck would have it, the party sighted the immense monster at dusk when they made camp. They recognized the horrifying sight as the carnivorous horned dinosaur called the Ceratosaurus. Fifty feet long and black in color, the dinosaur also sported coarse hair like that of a boar. The creature simply stared at the men as it feasted upon a caribou. As it did so, Leemore actually snapped a photo of the remnant dinosaur! Then, like a monstrous kangaroo, the creature bounded away into the night, leaving the hunters terrified and at a loss for what they had just seen.

Leemore, oddly enough, decided not to go public with their story or his photograph. Dupuy, though, went to the governor and requested men and supplies to go hunt the monster. After that, Dupuy briefly became the "laughing stock" of Dawson. And for a time, that was the end of the Ceratosaur's story.

Jumping ahead four years later, we find our friend George Dupuy covering the great Peking to Paris Race of 1907. The idea for the race had begun with a challenge issued via the Paris newspaper *Le Matin* on January 31, 1907, stating, "What needs to be proved today is that as long as a man has a car, he can do anything and go anywhere. Is there anyone who will undertake to travel this summer from Peking to Paris by automobile?"

The race exploded from the French embassy in Peking on June 10th that same year and concluded on August 10th. The winner was Prince Scipione Borghese, a friend of the Duke of Westminster, among others. Somehow the subject of Dupuy's dinosaur sighting was breached as he talked to one of the men. This ignited the interest of the Duke, who wanted to know more. Fatefully, not long after on Christmas Eve of that same year, Father Lavagneux and several Indians spotted the monster yet again. He sent a letter to Dupuy about it, who himself then showed the Duke. Serious plans were made to head to the Yukon in 1908, and newspapers reported that the Duke and his bride were coming to America for an extended vacation in June.

ICE AGE

SCENE FROM THE 1907
PEKING TO PARIS RACE.

However, this planned hunting trip of the Duke's didn't happen. Though an exact reason as to why is unknown, it is a fact that the Duke competed in the London Olympics as a motorboat racer in the summer of 1908. Presumably, this took precedence over his dinosaur hunt. For the next four years there was no mention of another hunt—at least to this author's knowledge—until 1912 when a special German tramp steamer was chartered at Hamburg. It had a special cargo hold eighty feet long, thirty feet high, and twenty feet wide to contain the monster. The plan was to capture the beast and take it back to London![6]

And then World War I happened. Unlike some royal lords, the Duke of Westminster fought on the front lines and even developed an armored Rolls-Royce car! So, once again, his trip to the Yukon was postponed. It's unknown if the Duke ever resumed plans to hunt the monster prior to 1927, but that year the creature was back in the headlines. This time the monster was sighted in a newly discovered mountain range in Siberia! The theory was that when the Bering Strait froze over, the beast crossed it into Russia. Writer Sterling Heilig, who had written the articles ten years previous, implied in his new article that a French sportsman called Lelvouier "the un-killable" was trying to convince the Duke and his friends that it would be possible

---

[6] This plan to bring the monster to London predates the 1925 film adaptation of *The Lost World*, for anyone who may have drawn a connection there. Furthermore, that plot development was unique to the film and no brontosaurus is brought to London in the book version.

ICE AGE

to drive across the Bering Strait. If the Duke ever saw the monster is unknown, but it is said that the Duke gave a description of the animal somewhere, which was later reprinted in *Coronet Magazine* in 1961.

What I just gave you above is a very short primer for the unabridged firsthand accounts. The first was written by George Dupuy in April of 1908 for *The Strand Magazine,* while many of the rest were articles written by reporter Sterling Heilig. With no further ado, here is Dupuy's firsthand account as published in *The Strand*.

"The Monster of Partridge Creek."
By GEORGES DUPUY.

M. Georges Dupuy, the well-known French writer and traveler, who has made many explorations in the Polar regions, here relates a most extraordinary experience which befell him in the frozen steppes of Alaska. M. Dupuy, whose good faith is beyond question, takes full responsibility for his narrative, which is, it may be noted, however remarkable, in no way contradicted by known scientific facts. The drawings which accompany this article have been made from sketches and descriptions supplied by M. Dupuy.

The story which follows is in no sense a romance. I wish, in the first place, to ask the readers of the following narrative to believe that I am in no way attempting to impose upon their credulity. Concerning the amazing spectacle I am about to describe, I report nothing but plain facts, however astounding and apparently incredible they may seem at first glance, precisely as they appeared to my own eyes—and I am possessed of excellent sight—and to those of my three companions —all three white men—without counting five Indians of the Klayakuk tribe, who have their camps on the shores of the River Stewart.

The following are the names of the three ocular witnesses who are ready to testify to the truth of my assertions: the first is my hunting companion for many years, Mr. James Lewis Buttler, banker, of San Francisco; the second is Mr. Tom Leemore, miner, from McQuesten River, in the Yukon Territory; and lastly, the Reverend Father Pierre Lavagneux, a Canadian Frenchman and missionary at the Indian village of Armstrong Creek, not far from McQuesten.

In the course of ten years' rambling in the four quarters of the world it has been my lot to witness a great number of amazing spectacles, and the strange experience of which I speak had become no more than a vivid recollection when, a few days ago — on January 24th, 1908 — the following letter reached me at Paris. It came from Father Lavagneux, who passes his life with his savage flock six hundred miles north west of the Klondike. I give it here word for word:

Armstrong Creek,
January 1st, 1908.

ICE AGE

My Dear Son,

The 'trader' of McQuesten has just stopped here with his train of dogs and sledges. He has had a hard journey from Dawson, by Barlow, Flat Creek, and Dominion. I expect to receive by him in another fortnight fresh provisions and news of the outside world. Today is the first day of the New Year, and I want this letter to express my affectionate wishes for your health and happiness. I hope it will give me the pleasure of receiving you under my humble roof, here, at the other end of the earth. I will not believe that you will let your old friend in the Great North leave his old carcass to the Indians (who will someday or other make his coffin out of branches) without seeing him once more.

I have received your book, the reading of which has given me the greatest pleasure. By the way, you are wrong in regard to that poor fellow, John Spitz. Alas! He is no longer mail-carrier of the Duncan district. He died, poor fellow, at Eagle Camp, soon after you departed, not having survived the wound he received from the 'bald-face,' which you will remember.

Talking of ferocious animals, will you believe me when I tell you that ten of my Indians and myself saw again, on Christmas Eve, that horrible beast of Partridge Creek passing like a whirlwind over the frozen surface of the river, breaking off with his hind feet enormous blocks of ice from the rough surface? His fur was covered with hoar frost, and his little eyes gleamed like fire in the twilight. The beast held in his jaws something which seemed to me to be a caribou. It was moving at the rate of more than ten miles an hour. The temperature that day was forty-five degrees below zero. At the corner of the 'cut-off' it disappeared. It is undoubtedly the same animal that we saw before. Accompanied by Chief Stineshane and two of his sons I followed the traces, which were exactly like those which we all saw— Leemore, Buttler, you, and I—in the mud of the ' moose-lick.' Six times, on the snow, we were able to measure the impression of its enormous body, the same size as we found it before, almost to the twentieth of an inch. We followed them to Stewart, fully two miles, when the snow began to fall slightly and blotted out the traces."

It was on receipt of this letter that I decided to write the story of my own experience, which it recalled so vividly to mind, and of which it afforded a striking confirmation.

The Story of My Friend Buttler

The station of McQuesten, that far-off corner of the strange country of the Yukon, where the eight months of winter are so terrible but the short summer so marvelously beautiful, was on four occasions my chosen retreat during the eight years that I have known the North. A

ICE AGE

friend of mine in San Francisco, Mr. Buttler, who had come to Dawson City in order to purchase gold mining concessions, had promised to join me in order that we should go hunting together. I was taking my coffee one afternoon in the veranda of Father Lavagneux's cabin when all at once I heard someone whistle from the farther bank of the river. A bark canoe, paddled by two Indians, was coming up the river in the shadow of the trees. Buttler was with them.

"My dear fellow," he said, smiling as I met him, and endeavoring to hide his visible agitation, "I have something very strange to tell you. Do you know that prehistoric monsters still exist? "

I broke out laughing, and together we returned by the little path which led to the Father's house. When Buttler had taken off his muddy boots and was ensconced in a comfortable seat he began to recount his story as follows: "Leaving Gravel Lake, where I arrived on Tuesday evening, my last stage was the mouth of Clear Creek, where I knew that you would send someone to meet me. Travelling was frightfully bad—forty miles of marshy country. At last, at nightfall, I descended a hill, and had the pleasure of seeing Grant's cabin, which was lighted up. Grant was at home, and a good supper was waiting for me. Early the next morning (yesterday) he came to tell me, in his reserved and silent manner, that three fine moose were feeding quietly behind the plateau

COWBOYS & SAURIANS

"THE DINOSAURUS!—IT IS THE DINOSAURUS OF THE ARCTIC"

of Partridge Creek. After swallowing a hasty mouthful all four of us—Grant, your two men, and I—started out from the hut. We made a wide detour. At the top of a hill, where we had hidden ourselves, all of us stretched full length on the ground, we perceived, a short distance off in the valley, near a 'moose-lick,' three enormous moose moving slowly forward and quietly browsing on the moss and lichens. All at once they gave three simultaneous bounds, and,

ICE AGE

"CIRCLE! MUTTERED FATHER LAVAGNEUX, WITH CHATTERING TEETH."

one of the males giving vent to the striking bellow which these animals utter only when they are hunted or mortally wounded, the three went off at a mad gallop towards the south.

"What had happened?"

"We decided to approach the spot where the animals had taken fright so suddenly. Arriving at the 'moose-lick,' a spot about sixty feet long and fifteen wide, we saw in the mud, and almost on a level with the water of the 'moose-lick,' the fresh imprint of the body of a monstrous animal. Its belly had made an impression in the slime more than two feet deep, thirty feet long, and twelve feet wide. Four gigantic paws, also deeply impressed, had left at each end of the main imprint, and a little to the side, footprints five feet long by two and a half feet wide, the claws being more than a foot long, the sharp points of which had buried themselves deeply in the mud. There was also the print, apparently, of a heavy tail, ten feet long and sixteen inches wide at the point.

"We followed the tracks of the monster in the valley for five or six miles, and then, at the ravine of Partridge Creek—a place which the miners call a gulch—they ceased suddenly as if by enchantment."[7]

How the Monster Appeared to Us

The next day, at five o'clock in the morning, Father Lavagneux, Buttler, Leemore, a neighbouring miner hastily summoned, myself, and five men of the tribe, crossed the River Stewart in two canoes. Neither of the first two guides, who were overcome with terror, nor the sergeant of the Mounted Police, who received

---

[7] This might be a relevant place to interject that the Burrunjor, a Tyrannosaurus cryptid in Australia, occasionally vanishes into thin air when sighted by witnesses. Tracks of the animal also occasionally vanish suddenly without a trace. Australian cryptozoologist Rex Gilroy has since theorized that these dinosaur cryptids are victims of time displacement, and are not "prehistoric survivors" so to speak.

ICE AGE

our story with skepticism, nor the letter-carrier, would consent to accompany us.

All day long we searched, without result, the valley of the little River McQuesten, the flats of Partridge Creek, and the country between Harlow and the lofty, snow-covered mountains.

At last, towards evening, tired out, after having toiled for a long time through the great marsh, we lighted a fire at the top of a rocky ravine. The sun was setting. Lying by the fire we let our eyes wander over the glittering expanse of marsh which we had just traversed.

The tea was boiling and everyone was preparing to dip his tin cup into the pot, when suddenly a noise of rolling stones and a strange, harsh, and frightful roar made us all spring to our feet.

The beast for which we had been looking—a black, gigantic form, the corners of his mouth filled with blood-stained slime, his jaws munching something, I know not what—was slowly and heavily climbing the opposite side of the ravine, making the large boulders roll into the valley as he went!

Struck with terror, Father Lavagneux, Leemore, and myself tried to utter a cry of fright, but no sound issued from our parched throats. Unconsciously we had seized each other's arms. The five Indians were crouching down with their faces against the ground, trembling like leaves shaken by the wind. Buttler was already rushing down the hill.

"The dinosaurus!—it is the dinosaurus of the Arctic Circle!" muttered Father Lavagneux, with chattering teeth.

The monster had stopped scarcely twenty paces from us, and, resting upon his huge belly, was staring, motionless, at the red sun, which was bathing all the landscape in a weird light.

For a full ten minutes, riveted to the spot by some strange force which we could not overcome, did we contemplate this terrible apparition.

We were, however, in full possession of all our senses. There was not, and never will be, in our minds the least doubt as to the reality of what we saw. It was indeed a living creature, and not an illusion, which we had before us.

The dinosaurus then turned his immense neck, but did not seem to see us. His withers were at least eighteen feet above the ground. His entire body from the extremity of his yawning jaws—which were surmounted by a horn like that of a rhinoceros—to the end of the tail must have measured at least fifty feet. His hide was like that of a wild boar, garnished with thick bristles, in colour a greyish-black. His belly was plastered with thick mud.

At this moment Buttler returned to us. He told us that he thought the animal weighed about thirty tons.

Suddenly the dinosaurus moved his jaws, visibly chewing some thick viscid kind of food, and we heard a sound like that of the crunching of small bones. Then, with a sudden movement,

ICE AGE

he raised himself on his hind legs, and giving utterance to a roar—a hollow, indescribable, frightful sound—and wheeling round with surprising agility, with movements resembling those of a kangaroo, he sprang with a prodigious bound into the ravine.

On the 24th, Buttler and myself, having taken two days' rest, started for Dawson City, for the purpose of demanding from the Governor fifty armed men and mules.

Here my story ends. For a month we were the laughingstock of the Golden City, and the Dawson Daily Nugget published an article about me, which was at the same time flattering and satirical, entitled "A Rival of Poe".

In retrospect, Dupuy's account is odd compared to the newspaper articles published later. One may have noticed that Dupuy says nothing of Leemore snapping a photo of the monster, a very significant detail not revealed until an article published only a month after this one. As to why, one could argue that Leemore and Dupuy had agreed to not show the photograph to anyone. Leemore felt it best to obtain the financing of a rich sportsman so that they could mount a proper expedition to find the creature. So, we may surmise that Dupuy intentionally left out the fact that a photograph was taken as he did not yet have the backing to finance a monster hunt. If this was the case, he need not have worried, for only a month later news began being reported regarding the Duke of Westminster's impending monster hunt. The

Baltimore Sun from May 10, 1908, reported the following:

Gigantic Keratosaurus, Seventy Feet In Length, Found ALIVE In Alaskan Backwoods

Four Men, Including A Priest, See It And One Of Them Snapshot It. Young Duke Of Westminster Finances An Expedition Which Will Search For It. Enormous Monster Is Probable Sole Survivor Of Species Which Roamed North America A Million Years Ago.

THE ONLY KERATOSAURUS YET ALIVE ON EARTH

Its head, when it stands erect, is 40 feet in the air.

It is strong enough to run off with a 700-pound buck.

It is 70 feet long and its body is covered with long gray-black hair.

It travels at the rate of 40 miles an hour.

Paris, April 27.—The antediluvian Keratosaurus of the Arctic Circle is alive and plans to capture him are being made.

This is why the millionaire young Duke of Westminster is now in conference in Paris.

ICE AGE

This also explains why he will visit the United States in June.

In London they say vaguely that the Duke and fair young Dutchess are due "a long American vacation." "Just what are their plans nobody seems to know," admitted the cables, "but undoubtedly the richest peer and peeres in England will receive unusual social attentions, while the Duke will take a hunting trip in the Rockies."

In Paris we know the sensational secret motive of the Rocky Mountain expedition, which will quietly extend the way up to the McQuesten River, in the Yukon, where the Klayakuk tribe of the Snow Indians wait close-mouthed and patient, around the Canadian posts of Armstrong creek until the good Jesuit father Lavagnneux shall give the word, "They come!"

In San Francisco, too, there is a man who knows the banker, James L. Butler. Long before the Duke's party comes he will be strangely busy at the railway and the waterfront receiving stores and Hamburg cablegrams and testing silent, fearless men, who take cash in advance and asked no questions.

And there is a miner of the Yukon—Tom Leemore—who, with George Dupuy and James Butler and the Jesuit father, saw the Keratosaurus in its rage and photographed it in its rampage when it flicked an avalanche of great rocks down and around their heads.

COWBOYS & SAURIANS

TO CATCH THE CRITTER

Who has seen the photographs of the Partridge Creek monster? Not the Dawson authorities, who refuse to lend 100 meals and 50 armed men to go hunting. Not the editor of the Daily Nugget, who dubbed George Dupuy "a Rival of Edgar Poe."

The miner, Leemore, who remained at Armstrong Creek, pigheadedly confided them to Father Lavagneux alone—"to interest some rich and serious French or English sport," and now that George Dupuy is back in Paris with the Duke of Westminster behind him one of the most extraordinary photographs on earth is in the young Duke's pocket, while Dupuy has in *his* pocket a liberal contract to indemnify all those concerned and fit an expedition that must include a 4000 ton tramp steamer—to bring straight to London the live monster, weighing 80 tons and more.

The Duke of Westminster has also in his pocket the following letter from the Jesuit missionary to George Dupuy after his return to Paris. It enclosed the photograph:

I want to stop and interrupt the newspaper article for a moment to say that what follows is a different translation of Father Lavagneux's letter. As such, it is the same information all over again, only translated in a different way. As I'm sure some readers are interested enough to see the differences, I have included it. Furthermore, the rest of the article is another retread of the original

ICE AGE

sighting, but with additional details which I shall embolden for you. I have mostly included the full article in the interest of historical preservation, and to serve as a resource for those who have a deep interest in the story. If you have only a passing interest, I would suggest you only read the emboldened text within the reprint.

The Monster, from the Alleged Photograph Taken of the Creature.

ARMSTRONG CREEK CANADIAN POST

January 1, 1908

My Dear *Boy*: The McQueston trader has arrived, with sledge and dogs. He will make the hard trip to Dawson by the Barlow, Flat Creek and Dominion. **On his return I shall have fresh food and news from the world, and I hope from your dear self, with the word from Leemore, who, you will see by the precious photograph herewith, deems the time right before your best effort. Entrusting** the proof to you, he stipulates * * * (business) * * *[8]

What joy will it not give me to receive you again under my roof, here at the world's end? Because I will not believe you could permit your friend of the great North to give up his old carcass to the branch coffins of the Stewart Indians without visiting him once more.

I have your book. Its reading captivated me incredibly; but you err as to poor John Spitz. He is no longer mail carrier. He died at Eagle's Camp from the wounds given him by the "bald face" (grizzly) you know of * * *

And now, would you believe, in the name of our Lord, that I and 10 of my Indians again saw Christmas afternoon Leemore's terrible monster?

It passed like a hurricane across the frozen river, smashing, dashing, crashing immense blocks of broken ice into the air behind it. All its long bristles were covered with hoarfrost, and its red eyes flamed in the twilight.

The monster held in its mouth a caribou that weighed at least 700 pounds, while it careered along at 20 miles an hour. At the corner of the cut off it disappeared.

In company with Chief Stineshame and two of his sons I took [note] of its tracks,

---

[8] This is exactly how the letter appears in the paper.

exactly as you, Butler, Leemore and I did that last day in the moose leak.

Now my son, Leemore insists that * * * (business) * * *

The present writer has copied a copy of the letter. There may be omissions—added words; of course, it is translation also, but as to the substantial accuracy of everything touching the existence of the monster I am positive there is no error of copying or translation.

ABOUT GEORGES DUPUY
The positive good faith of Georges Dupuy is also beyond doubt in Paris, where he is well known. His place as a writer and sporting Explorer is quite fixed.

When the New York - Paris automobile race was being organized his mere word convinced Parisians of the impossibility of crossing Bering Strait upon the ice - which don't exist. Three times in the last eight years Dupuy has made long visits to the Klondike, always as a sport with money.

James Lewis Buttler, his friend and San Francisco banker, being up at Dawson buying gold claims last July, sent word to Dupuy he would meet him at McQueston Post for a week's hunting.

Taking his coffee on the porch of Father Lavagneux the French sport perceived Butler hurrying to him from the birchbark canoe and two Indians Father Lavagneux had sent to meet him. Butler was much agitated.

"Do you know that there are prehistoric monsters alive up here?" were his first words.

Laughing, Dupuy led the banker inside to the Jesuit, but when he saw Father Lavagneux received the story with grave faith he laughed no longer.

"Gravel Lake, my last camp, was to be the mouth of Clear creek, where I would meet your men," said Butler. "It was terrible going—40 miles of swamp. At night, therefore, I joyfully perceived Grant's cabin lights. He gave me a good supper.

"At 5 P. M. Grant came, announcing in his furtive way three big moose back of Partridge Creek. He, your two Indians and I saw the moose. They had been quietly feeding. Suddenly the male let out the bellow that means fright, and off they went at breakneck speed. What could it be?

"We hurried up to the moose leak and saw.

"A prodigy stared us in the face.

"Fresh in the mud was the print of a monster body. The belly had made a gully 2 feet deep, 30 feet long and 12 feet wide. Four gigantic feet—a yard by half a yard and claws 12 inches long—had made a lot of prints.

"**And, horrifying above all, was a vast pile of greenish-wine-colored manure, smoking fresh, two yards cube. It was the excrement of no possible living animal—and not produced by the digestion of vegetable matter.**"

ICE AGE

Grant and Butler followed the tracks three miles to "the gulf," a dark and rocky ravine, where they disappeared.

"What do you think of that?" concluded Butler.

FACED THE HUGE BRUTE.
At 5 o'clock the next morning Father Lavagneux, Dupuy, Butler and Leemore, the only miner except Grant (who refused to join the hunt), went to the tracks, accompanied by five Indians. Neither the sergeant of the mounted police nor the trader would have anything to do with it.

"We tramped the flats of Partridge Creek in vain that morning," says Dupuy. "At noon we built a fire in a big rocky ravine. We had almost given up expecting anything. Then, as the tea was boiling, down came crashing an avalanche of boulders, amid roarings, snorting, rumblings and thunderous windbreakings that made the earth tremble.

"The Thing was upon us in an instant. The monster, black, gigantic. Its chops dripping bloody lather with a sickening noise of mastication, punctuated by the deafening claps of a Titanic colic, lurched down the ravine—beyond us—sweeping rocks aside like pebbles.

"Father Lavagneux and I were petrified. The Indians lay upon their bellies.

"A Keratosaurus! The Keratosaurus of the Arctic Circle alive!" babbled Father Lavagneux as the outrageous Thing stopped and stared at us with disdainful curiosity.

"For 10 long minutes, nailed to the spot, we stared at the prehistoric creature. It stared at us. In full daylight."

"You have seen the Eiffel Tower? In the same manner I have seen the Keratosaurus.

"Its withers stood 25 feet high. Its entire body—from rhinoceros horn to tail tip—must have measured 70 feet. Its hide was like that of the wild boar, covered with two-foot long bristles, gray-black.

"From its hairy belly hung clods of mud as big as a 10-year-old child.

SNAPPED HIS KODAK.
"The noise of its mastication—crackling bones—was like the grinding of ice in a debacle. That of its indigestion was like when a hurricane tears the shrouds out of a big schooner! Its stench overpowered us...

"Then suddenly it raised its head, shook the hills with a long roar and romped down the ravine in gigantic bounds at 40 miles per hour. Its head, held 40 feet above the ground, was the last thing I saw in the whirlwind of rocks hell-racketing behind it!

"No use to shoot at such a fellow," Dupuy heard a casual voice behind him monologing. "But I got three snapshots at him with my faithful kodak, the sun well upon my back. Just my luck to have only three films in it!"

ICE AGE

It was Leemore, the most phlegmatic temperament Dupuy has ever run across while others were transfixed with horror. Leemore was already calculating what he could make from his snapshots.

"If I take them into Dawson," he said later, in reply to all appeals for proofs, "one of two things will happen. Either those 'smart-alecs' will give us the laugh for faking photos, or there's just a possibility the whole town will turn out to hunt the Ker—at—

"O saurus."

"Thanks. Where will we be? No, we'll keep quiet about it. Father Lavagneux and Dupuy, sport, will use the photographs to interest one of those game English earls with millions, who'll be glad to fit a proper expedition and square us in a proper lordly manner!"

These are the facts that are leading up to the Duke of Westminster's "American vacation" that begins next June.

Leemore was right in his surmise, first to last.

"On the 24th of the month," says Dupuy, "Butler and I went down to Dawson.[9] We asked the Governor for 50 armed mules and 100 men. For 30 days we were the laughing stock of Dawson city, and the *Nugget* published on myself the flattering editorial that had for title: 'A Rival of Edgar Poe.'"

---

[9] Evidently, their excitement got the better of them and they talked.

COWBOYS & SAURIANS

At this hour, even while they fit the expedition out, neither Dupuy nor the young Duke will be disturbed that I have told the bare outline of their great project.

"No one will believe it," said the Duke last night, while dining at Paillard's. [I was not present.]

No one will believe that they are chartering a German tramp at Hamburg...with the privilege of tearing out of it a central steel-grilled space 60 feet long, 25 feet wide and 30 feet deep. What for? What do you think? To bring back gold?

AN AMERICAN IN PARIS

The article had some other interesting deviations aside from the revelation that Leemore took a photo (which Lavagneux now mentions in his letter, a detail Dupuy omitted). Notably, this version claims that the monster (now 70 feet long rather than 50) stared at the men, while Dupuy's article claimed that the beast didn't even notice them.

ICE AGE

An abbreviated variation of the article printed in the *Monmouth Morning Gazette* on June 16th compared the Duke to King George about to slay a dragon. There was no new information reported, however, so we shall not recount it.

The next article I found is somewhat satirical and mostly pokes fun at the Duke of Westminster and spends very little time on the monster itself. The article, from the *Brisbane Worker* on July 18, 1908, goes thusly:

Prehistoric Monsters

Recent explorers bring hair raising reports of a frightening beast roaming the Arctic circle, seeking whom it may devour.

This is how Georges Dupuy, a credible witness, describes it:

The monster, black and gigantic, lurched down the ravine beyond us, sweeping great rocks aside like pebbles.

We were petrified. For 10 minutes we stared at the prehistoric thing. Its withers stood 25 feet high. From its nose to its tail of the Titanic monster measured 70 feet, and as it crashed over the ground its head was held 60 feet high in the air. Then suddenly it raised its head and roared like thunder, and went romping down the ravine in vast abounds at 40 miles an hour.

> How much of a stir Dupuy's story caused at the time is unknown, but one man who read and critiqued Dupuy's article at the time was none other than Richard Lydekker, the English naturalist and geologist. He had this to say in the September 1908 issue of *Knowledge & Illustrated Scientific News* (Vol. 5 no. 9.):
>
> **"The Monster of Partridge Creek"**
> That a living representative of the carnivorous dinosaurs of the Secondary Epoch should be living in the frozen North of Alaska seems incredible to every scientific mind, and yet, if it does not, why on earth should an apparently respectable French writer and traveler, as well as a French-Canadian priest commit deliberate perjury? I allude of course, to an article with the same heading as this paragraph, in the July number of the *Strand Magazine*. The prima *facie* presumption is that the larger dinosaurs were inhabitants of warm rather than of Arctic zones. The creature is stated to have been seen carrying off in its mouth an animal which appeared to be a reindeer (caribou). The artist has, however, represented it with a deer, whose horns seem in some degree intermediate between those of a sambur and those of a red deer; but, then, artists generally do their best to distort zoological facts!
>
> This was all Lydekker had to say on the matter, and though he poked fun at the artist's work in the article, it would seem he doesn't entirely dismiss the story, which is rather interesting.

What is it? The Keratosaurus—an animal hitherto thought to exist only in fossil remains—a hideous survival from a bygone period.

An expedition is being fitted out by the Duke of Westminster, regardless of cost, to capture the brute alive and bring it to London and

ICE AGE

people are amazed at the zeal his Lordship is exhibiting in the chase.

It does seem rather strange, but Dukes being themselves survivals from an antediluvian age, it may be that an instinctive sense of kinship has something to do with the case.

The ducal tribe, though degenerate, are even now, of a devouring capacity unequaled in the present day jungle, and it is possible that the Keratosaurus will furnish them with hints of an ancestry more remote than is dreamt of in the College of Harold's.

Why bring it to London, though, which already has too many prehistoric monsters of its own?

There would be more sense a proposal to take the Duke of Westminster, and the whole menagerie of the House of Lords, contact them off to join the Keratosaurus in the Frozen Zone.

There were other articles too, though they shall not be reprinted in full, and only the relevant bits will be covered.

For instance, this article from the *Daily Kennebec Journal* on Wednesday, May 20, 1908, adds in yet another new detail that explosive bullets are being made to hunt the monster in the following paragraph:

The authorities for the story are a French missionary, a goldminer and about half a dozen Indians. This missionary claims to have photographed the great beast and to prove his assertions has sent a remarkable picture of a lizard-like creature of enormous proportions to a friend in Paris, who, in turn, has given the likeness to the Duke of Westminster. This, together with a letter from the priest, is said to have convinced the young Englishman, and according to a dispatch from Paris, he at present is arranging with a French firm for supplies and specially bored rifles which will carry explosive bullets weighing a half pound apiece.

As to a bit more on the photographs, an article in the *Queanbeyan Age* from Tuesday, July 28, 1908, attests that, "The miner Leemore took three snapshots of the creature, prints of which the 'Record Herald' correspondent asserts are in the possession of the Duke of Westminster."

News of the monster died down at the onset of World War I, and then flared up again in the mid-1920s.

THE ANACONDA STANDARD, SUNDAY, OCTOBER 28, 1923.

Prehistoric Monster Still Haunts Arctic

By STERLING HEILIG.

The antediluvian Keratosaurus of the Arctic Circle is alive and may be run down in automobiles by the plain tracks he is making in extreme Northeast Siberia!

So say the Soviet papers.

ICE AGE

Traveling back and forth over certain districts in Kamtchatka the prehistoric monster and his family have been "breaking veritable roads," which "apparently lead to Bering Strait."

A photograph (a veritable photograph) is circulating which indicates a family of them. It shows the claw, or foot of "a very young Keratosaurus," whose mangled remains were found by natives along the route. Yet the baby claw is big enough to enclose the head of a large man. A drawing of the full sized creature "from descriptions of eyewitnesses" suggests the bulk of five elephants.

Keratosaurus and his route across Bering Strait on the ice are inclined to be credited by French sportsmen who believed (and still believe) in the Partridge Creek monster of the Yukon, which they came near to hunting in a great Anglo-French expedition just before the war. "The Keratosaurus of the Arctic Circle" is the sensational survival's name; and the new Soviet story fits in with its periodic disappearance from Alaska.

When Diomede Freezes Over.
It crosses Bering Strait, they say, in years when ice freezes between the Diomede Islands. And a few years before the war those same French sportsmen were arranging to get up an all land automobile race from Paris to New York over that same Far North stamping ground where the Keratosaurus family are now breaking roads.

COWBOYS & SAURIANS

They were not visionary theorists. They had just done Paris-Peking. Prince Scipione Borghese, who won Paris-Peking, entered immediately for Paris-New York. The unkillable Lelouvier (along with Goddard) was attacked by escaped Siberian convicts on the edge of the Gobi desert. Goddard was never seen again: and Lelouvier was left for dead. But along came an Imperial postal relay twenty hours behind its schedule. It transported Lelouvier, inert, to Omsk, where Mlle. Kreiss, goddaughter of the Governor of Irkutsk, helped nurse him back to life—and finally eloped with him from Verkhoiansk, "the coldest town in the Old World" in a specially equipped motor car— over equivalently the worst section of the Bering Strait trip.

Another great French sport was Georges Dupuy, the veteran correspondent of the *Auto*, sporting daily of Paris, who brought back more than the full story of the Keratosaurus from Alaska. There, seeking facts about the Alaskan route for Paris-New York, he "played faro bank on the Ice of Bering Sea, two miles off shore, in front of Nome City. The game was running in the Monte Carlo Casino, built of pine logs calked with tow. Ten red hot stoves made the establishment warm for the gambling miners and young ladies of Nome City dance halls, whose smart sled teams of Eskimo dogs waited for them at the door.

"Just before twilight," told Dupuy, "some two miles or less distant, we could see the little blue waves out there in Bering Sea. Not once did it freeze more than five miles out, at Nome. But there are periods when the strait freezes. One year thirty-six whaling ships were abandoned in the ice, the crews escaping afoot with sledges."

Above all, what Dupuy brought back—and dropped all else to bring—were proofs, plans and undertakings of American and Canadian eyewitnesses to join an expedition to hunt "the Partridge Creek monster."

He had even a snapshot photograph of it.

The Duke of Westminster was interested by the photograph and finally decided by correspondence of a Franco-English combination with the San Francisco banker, James L. Butler. An ostensible shooting trip would quietly extend to the McQueston River, in the Yukon, where the Klayakuk tribe of the Snow Indians waited around the Canadian post of Armstrong Creek until the good Jesuit Father Lavagneux should give the word: "They come!"

From here, the article is more or less a reprint of the earlier piece, the only additional detail being that one of Leemore's photos didn't turn out as he remarks, "I got three snapshots at him with my Kodak. Just my luck I had only three films and one of 'em is budged."

To jump ahead back to the relevant pieces of the article:

Which facts led to the interest of the Duke of Westminster. The expedition, slowly and carefully planned, with three French sports and twice as many English, dragged through correspondence, summer after summer. Tom Leemore, the miner, Grant, the Indian and Father Lavagneaux (for the work of his mission) received periodical remittances of ample proportions, which made them patient.

In 1912 a German tramp steamer was chartered at Hamburg—with the privilege of clearing out of it, from hold up, a central space (to be steel grilled) eighty feet long, thirty feet high and twenty feet wide. What for? What do you think? To bring back gold? The contract for this cage was given out and stores, munitions and peculiar motor cars specially designed for their purpose were ready to load when the cage should be in place.

Then came the war.

It ended everything.

The K. Is Offered as Bait.

And now the Soviets (war's sinister product), having no use personally for their Keratosaurus family, offer it as bait to the averted and reproving West—a new temptation to resume relations.

Lenine, Trotzky & Co. are subtle psychologists. France might forget a quantity of lost investments for the privilege to hunt a veritable prehistoric—what? Jurassic!—monster over new tracked snow from the old Paris-Peking routs.

Lelouvier (who knows the ground, none better) claims it to be absolutely feasible to

ICE AGE

motor in new, modern equipped cars right up to Bering Strait

He recalls his trip with his runaway bride in a 40 horsepower automobile of the 1906 model!

"Over the hard snow and ice bound rivers, from Verkholansk to Yakoutsk, steering by compass mostly, no roads being visible, was like speeding on a smooth race track. Not once did we have a puncture or a blowout. In such cold, the motor, never heating, gives its full force without loss by evaporation or danger of gripping.

"With a modern 30 horsepower, or even 20 horsepower, equipped interiorly in the style of my benefactor, the Siberian Prince. I guarantee carrying supplies for it from station to station as far as 1,000 miles apart!"

The Siberian Prince (alas!) has been lost in the shuffle. But the Soviets are quite as aristocratically liberal handed for those whom they would entice. The super hunt tempts French and British sports immensely. The Keratosaurus and his family are up there in Kamtchatka, "making their own roads to hunt them by!"

"In a winter climate that goes to 85 degrees below zero Fahrenheit it is a health and sporting trip," says Lelouvier, "to motor over the hard snow and ice. Infinite silence weighs over all. Nature sleeps. Rivers no longer flow. The sun moves round, at the height of a few degrees, clean cut and strong, without red halo. Through the pure, cloudless air the crow files weakly, leaving a light trail of vapor."

And, beneath, the Keratosaurus—on the job.

He sticks to a chosen route. He has his family breaking roads to Bering Strait, unconsciously, of course, but there you are! They may cross back this winter to Alaska if the ice holds. Any way, the Soviets affirm, the Keratosaurus leaves a plain road by which to be run down.

Paris-New York by land? The monsters found the route while men were fighting!

News was again silent for another four years until several articles appeared in 1927:

PREHISTORIC BEAST SEEN
Giant Saurian of Arctic Emerges
Siberians Report Monster Believed to Live in Cherski Range
Creature Once Hunted Over Alaska Now Exciting Russ Savants

Los Angeles Times, December 4, 1927
Paris, Dec 3. (Exclusive) "And now, will you believe, in the name of our Lord, that I and ten of my Indians saw again, on Christmas afternoon, Lemoore's terrible monster"?

"As big as ten elephants, it passed like a hurricane across the frozen river, smashing immense blocks of thick ice into the air. Its long bristles were covered with hoar-frost and its immense red eyes flamed in the twilight. The monster held in its mouth a caribou of close to 700 pounds, while it careened at twenty miles per hour!"

Such are the first mention and first description—both from Alaska—of the Keratosaurus of the Arctic Circle, gigantic prehistoric creature that's now again exciting Russian sports-men and scientists, along with the discovery of an unsuspected mountain range in Northeastern Siberia which may be its home.

SPECIAL EXPEDITIONS

Maps of Siberia will have to be changed by the discovery, only yesterday, of this newly named Cherski Range, 625 miles long, 180 miles wide, and covering an area greater than the Caucasus. It has been found by the explorer, Obruchev, sent by the Soviet government in 1926 to investigate the unknown regions beyond Yakutsk, east of the River Lena.

"This was probably the last great mountain range remaining to be uncovered on the globe," say the Russian papers. Will the Russian Geological Survey and Academy of Sciences, sending special expeditions to it, come on authentic facts about the giant saurian?

Of course, there seems to be no possibility of capturing a terrible monster "as big as ten elephants."

HUNTED IN ALASKA

To kill it, even, high explosive shells would be necessary, according to Lelouvler, who went out after the Keratosaurus in the first Russian excitement about ten years ago.

Lelouvier, "the un-killable," along with Prince Scipione Borghese and Goddard, had "done" Paris-Peking in specially-constructed motorcars. Another great sportsman was the French Georges Dupuy, veteran correspondent of the Paris Auto, who brought back the original full story of the Keratosaurus from Alaska, studied by Lelouvier and the others for their expedition.

The Duke of Westminster certainly believed in the "Partridge Creek Monster" and his Franco-English combination actually decided with a San Francisco banker named Butler that an ostensible shooting trip would quietly extend to the McQueston River in the Yukon, where the Klay-akuk Indians waited around the post of Armstrong creek until the good Jesuit Father Lavgneux should give the word "They come!"

SEEN WHILE RACING

Here came the first Alaskan story to Europe.

In particular, there was a miner of the Yukon, Tom Leemore, who—along with this Georges Dupuy, Banker Butler, and Father Lavagneux himself—beheld the Kerato-saurus in his rage, and photographed him when he kicked an avalanche of rocks close to their heads!

Pig-headedly, Leemore confided the print to Father Lavagneux alone, "to interest some rich and serious Eurpean sport." and insisted that "none of those Dawson crooks shall set eyes on it!"

ICE AGE

CARRIED CARIBOU
So the Duke of Westminster's friends had equally the account of how the monster was seen again with a caribou in its mouth. In the letter herein already quoted at the outset from the trustworthy Jesuit missionary to Georges Dupuy after the latter's return to Paris. If the great story is believable, it seems to have finally enclosed the photograph of Leemore!

Letter, photograph and good faith of Dupuy were never doubted in Paris. Three times, the sporting correspondent of the Auto visited the Klondike, and his tale was as follows:

Again, because the following portion is repetitive, I shall intercede and move us forward to the next relevant bit of the article.

BRUTE DISAPPEARES
...The monster disappeared from Alaska—the Duke of Westminster's combination never got at it.

Appearing soon after in Siberia, it would seem to travel back and forth across Behring Strait, when the ice is thick enough between the islands.

RANGE MAY BE HOME
How then, did the Keratosaurus equally disappear from Siberia, when Lelouvler and friends went after it? Some say, of course, that the prehistoric monster actually sleeps for ten-

year periods—being an astounding sole survivor in this manner!

VLADIMIR OBRUCHEV C. 1930s.

But, today, the Russians believe that the thing takes refuge in its real home—In the hitherto-unknown Cherski Range of mountains just discovered by Obruchev, official explorer sent into Unknown Siberia by the soviets.[10]

---

[10] Perhaps it's no coincidence that later in life Obruchev wrote several sci-fi novels, one of which portrayed dinosaurs surviving into the 20th Century. His novel *Plutonia* was written in 1915 and came out one year after Edgar Rice Burroughs's *At the Earth's Core*. Similar to that book,

ICE AGE

The Cherski Range, greater in area than the Caucasus, lies between East Siberia and the Pacific Coast adjoining Alaska. And the Keratossurus is again reported by Siberian natives. Just as the Cherski Mountains are discovered!

And this is the last we hear of our friend the Ceratosaurus, who we can presume lived out the rest of his days in Siberia. Having covered all of the articles, now onto a few questions, the first of which is: who was the writer Sterling Heilig? The book *Under Siege: Portraits of Civilian Life in France During World War I* had this to say about Heilig:

Born in 1864, Heilig graduated with a law degree from the University of Pennsylvania. His early career was spent in government secretarial posts including work in Europe. In 1892 he became a Paris-based correspondent for the *New York Sun*, and began syndicating "Paris-Illustrated" features for a variety of American Sunday newspapers. A founding member of the Anglo-American Press Association (1907), Heilig was a war correspondent on both the English and French fronts in 1914-1917, and then was accredited to the American Expeditionary Force in the last two years of the

---

explorers find an underground world (via an opening in the Arctic) full of Jurassic horrors—including a Ceratosaurus.

war. He spent the remainder of his career in France.[11]

If nothing else, Heilig certainly sounds reputable. And again, why write so many articles on a fake creature while using real figures in the story like the Duke of Westminster? Surely the real Duke would be incensed if Heilig were making up fantasies about him?

Those arguments aside, that's still not enough to lend the articles the credibility that they need. Upon closer examination, the stories have a lot going against them, their worst offense being that witnesses claimed the animal leaped like a kangaroo. As it was, the kangaroo was still a very exotic animal to foreigners in the early 1900s as it had only been scientifically classified in 1821. This ironically tied into the theories of some paleontologists in the mid-1800s. Specifically, in 1858, paleontologist Joseph Leidy theorized that the Hadrosaurus—a bipedal dinosaur—stood erect similar to a kangaroo and used its tail for balance. This idea was further capitalized on by well-known paleontologist Edward Drinker Cope in 1866. He went so far as to claim that the new dinosaur he discovered not only stood like a Kangaroo but probably hopped like one as well! This creature was called the Laelaps at the time and is today known as the Dryptosaurus. Artwork at the time by

---

[11] Young, *Under Siege: Portraits of Civilian Life in France During World War I*, pp.177.

ICE AGE

Cope himself depicted it in a kangaroo-like stance, which carried over to other dinosaurs as well.

COPE'S DEPICTION OF LAELAPS C.1869.

The kangaroo idea was challenged by Lois Dollo (who also correctly identified the stance of the Iguanodon), who tried his best to prove that bipedal dinosaurs were incapable of leaping like kangaroos.

Justin Mullis, religious studies scholar and an expert on crypto-fiction, had this to say when I showed him a proto version of this chapter:

Unfortunately, the idea [of dinosaurs exhibiting kangaroo behavior] didn't go away, because it had been replicated in art. Charles R. Knight, the most famous paleoartist of all time, worked with Cope and did a painting of two leaping Laelaps battling in 1897. In Dec. of 1900, artist Lawson Wood swipes Knight's Laelaps and puts them on the cover of *Pearson's Magazine*.

COWBOYS & SAURIANS

By 1905 swipes of Knight's art were showing up as far away as Germany on cards packaged with candies. And though it is after Dupuy's story, in 1912 Sir Arthur Conan Doyle puts leaping theropod dinosaurs in his novel *The Lost World*.

The fact that the Ceratosaurus in Dupuy's story jumps like a kangaroo, I would argue, is the strongest evidence for the story as a fabrication. It doesn't move like a real dinosaur. It moves like what people thought a theropod dinosaur would move like in the early 20th Century. That indicates that the story of the Partridge Creek Monster is not an account of someone's sighting of a dinosaur, but someone's imagining of one.[12]

Furthermore, the Ceratosaurus was a popular, well-known dinosaur in 1907. It had been discovered by a farmer named Marshall Parker Felch in 1883. In 1892, the first skeletal reconstruction of the animal was published, and in 1898, the skeleton was given to the Smithsonian National Museum of Natural History in Washington, D.C. Mullis tells me, "The first life reconstruction (i.e., illustration) was published in 1901, drawn by Joseph M. Gleeson under the supervision of acclaimed paleoartist Charles R. Knight."[13] This would have been six years before the alleged sighting in the Arctic Circle.

---

[12] Letter to the author.
[13] Ibid.

ICE AGE

GLEESON'S CERATOSAURUS C.1901.

Furthermore, like the Tombstone Pterodactyl of 1890, the Ceratosaurus's size was grossly exaggerated in the account. In real life, no skeletons over 20 feet long had ever been recovered, and the Yukon variety was over twice that size at 50 feet (or 70 depending on the source).

Another problem with the story is its initial publication in *Je sais tout* and *The Strand,* as both were famous for printing fictional stories...

On the other end of the spectrum, Dupuy's Ceratosaurus does exhibit some behaviors that went against the grain of what paleontologists believed in the early 20th Century that are accepted today. At the time, depicting a dinosaur that could survive in the snow would not have added any credibility to the story, as at that time, all scientists believed dinosaurs were cold-blooded. The idea that all dinosaurs were cold-blooded was abandoned by the 1970s, and by the 1990s, it was widely accepted that some dinosaurs were warmblooded.

Dupuy's next odd detail was that the Ceratosaurus had hair (which could have been

---

From the *Brainerd Daily Dispatch* on December 19, 1927

MISSED SOME GOOD HUNTING.

Captain William H. Fawcett, of Breezy Point Lodge near Brainerd, who spent some months hunting brown bear, mountain sheep, etc., in Alaska, missed the biggest name of all, it appears. According to a story from Paris a Keratosaurus is roaming the upper Yukon reaches.

The animal has been photographed by a Dawson miner, who admits he is a truthful man and who stood his ground while the monster, as big as ten elephants, was kicking loose an avalanche of rocks.

The gigantic prehistoric creature predates the glacial period and in some way appears to have survived that rush of ice and maintained its habitat near the Arctic circle.

The Keratosaurus kicks up quite a trail, making it easier to follow than a deer track. Its belly is reported to make a gully 4 feet deep, and perhaps 20 feet wide. Where it rested while feeding, it made an imprint 50 feet long. A foot print measured two yards across. On the hairy belly of this monster of Jurassic times hung clods of mud as big as 10-year-old children. When the animal is traveling high speed, it makes 20 miles an hour.

The average big game rifle of Captain Fawcett will not fell this monster and heavy artillery carrying explosive shells may be necessary. Science may demand that the Keratosaurus be preserved alive, but the capture of such a beast will present more problems than when the Captain's black bear ran away from Breezy Point.

ICE AGE

feathers misinterpreted as hair, too). Whether the dinosaur had feathers or hair, paleontologists of the time had not yet theorized that dinosaurs were capable of growing hair or feathers. All in all, this would seem an odd detail to add to the story if Dupuy wanted his story to be believable.

Stranger still, in 1981, scientists identified dinosaur bones which had been found in Alaska in the very early 1960s. What was strange was that the bones still seemed to be fresh. Furthermore, some of them were identified as belonging to a horned dinosaur. The find was reported in the *Geological Society of America Abstract Proceedings*, Vol. 17, on page 548 in 1985.

As for one final question, and one that certainly crossed my mind when reading the story: was taking a photo of an animal in the wild even possible back then? And why not publish the photo in the *Strand Magazine?*

First of all, it's most likely that Leemore used a No. 1 Brownie, which was manufactured in 1901. The camera was actually intended for children, and Eastman was surprised when adults began using the camera more than anyone else. Due to its small size and easy function, this is most likely, especially because Leemore mentions film in one of the articles. As to why it wasn't published in *The Strand* that is anyone's guess. My guess would be that the photo was so fuzzy that it probably could have been anything, especially since the sun was going down. However, back then, newspapers and magazines often were incapable of reproducing photographs, and often did so in the form of a drawing of the photograph.

Considering all of the facts, instead of a lost Thunderbird photo from Tombstone, Arizona, should we really be looking for a Ceratosaurus photo from the Yukon instead?

Sources:
Shuker, Karl. *Still In Search of Prehistoric Survivors.* Greeneville, OH: Coachwhip Publications, 2016.

Young, Robert J. *Under Siege: Portraits of Civilian Life in France During World War I.* Berghahn Books, 2000.

2
ATTACK OF THE GIANT BEAVERS
PREHISTORIC BEAVERS IN BEAR LAKE AND ELSEWHERE

IMAGINE A BEAVER DAM as big as a house. Now imagine a beaver as big as a bear. Yes, at one time, there were giant beavers. Their scientific name was *Castoroides ohioensis,* and it is believed they died out at the same time as the mammoths 10,000 years ago.[14] Like the other prehistoric monsters in this book, it would seem that a few of these giant beavers survived.

One of the earliest recorded sightings comes from Canada. In 1808, Alexander Henry the

---

[14] To be even more specific, there were two varieties that differed in size. *Castoroides ohioensis* was about the size of a black bear. It southern cousin, *Castoroides leiseyorum,* was slightly larger.

COWBOYS & SAURIANS

Younger was exploring the Red River in Manitoba. There he met a native Salteaux who told him a story of a giant beaver, which Henry recorded in his diary:

> A Salteaux, who I found here tented with the Courtes Oreilles, came to me this evening in a very ceremonious manner, and after having lighted and smoked his pipe informed me of his having been up a small river, a few days ago, upon a hunting excursion, when one evening while upon the water in his Canoe, watching the Beaver to shoot them, he was suddenly surprised by the appearance of a very large animal in the water. At first he took it for a Moose Deer, and was preparing to fire at it accordingly.
>
> But on its approach towards him he perceived it to be one of the Kitche Amicks or Large Beavers. He dare not fire but allowed it to pass on quite near his canoe without molesting it. I had already heard many stories concerning this large Beaver among the Saulteaux, but I cannot put any faith in them. Fear, I presume, magnifies an ordinary size Beaver into one of those monsters, or probably a Moose Deer or a Bear in the dark may be taken for one of them as they are seen only at night, and I am told they are very scarce.

Alexander Henry the Younger was no mere footnote in the history of the frontier, either. The man was one of the most significant fur trappers in

ICE AGE

Canada. From 1799 until his death in 1814, he kept the now-famous diary, which I just quoted from. Today it is considered to be one of the most valuable resources in the history of early day fur trappers.

A FUR TRADER IN CHIPEWYAN, ALBERTA, C. 1880s.

For those wondering if Younger's Beaver story was a "tall tale" crafted to fit prehistoric beavers, it cannot be. This is because the prehistoric beaver had yet to be discovered. Charles Fothergill, the British naturalist, heard Indian legends in Canada in 1816 of the animals and decided to search for bones of giant beavers—assuming, perhaps, that the legends were based upon fossils. However, it wasn't Fothergill who found the proof that giant beavers once existed, the bones were found by S.R. Hildreth in Nashport, Ohio, in 1837.

COWBOYS & SAURIANS

Nor were the Salteaux Indians of Canada the only North American tribes with stories of such creatures either. The Tlingit peoples in the vicinity of Sitka, Alaska, on Baranof Island have a legend of a giant beaver devastating an entire village! The Malecite tribe, along the St. John River near the borders of Quebec and New Brunswick have a story about a giant beaver monster that built a huge dam that blocked the river. The Pocumtuck Indian tribe in Massachusetts believed a giant beaver that ate people lived in Lake Hitchcock, a Pleistocene Epoch. In Cultus Lake in British Columbia is said to be yet another giant beaver living in the water.

There's even a theory that our friend, the Bear Lake Monster from Utah, is itself a giant beaver rather than a dinosaur. That, or a giant beaver also lives in the lake with a dinosaurian counterpart. Either way, a notable amount of accounts describe something like a giant beaver living in Bear Lake. The Ute Indians there had legends of a giant beaver eating a man near Pelican Point. The Shoshone likewise claim they saw a giant beaver in the Bear Lake Valley during the great snowstorm of 1830. Even one of the earliest monster sightings from a witness named Marion Thomas described something 20 feet long covered in "light brown fur like that of an otter" in an 1860 issue of *The Desert News*. After that, multiple witnesses observed a large brown monster followed by many more little monsters. The only problem with grouping the sighting into the giant beaver theory is the immense size of the animal that was sighted.

ICE AGE

GIANT BEAVERS BY CHARLES R. KNIGHT.

On Sunday, July 22, 1868, the *Desert News* reported on the sighting:

> [The witnesses'] attention was suddenly attracted to a peculiar motion or wave in the water, about three miles distant. The lake was not rough, only a little disturbed by a light wind. Mr. Slight says he distinctly saw the side of a very large animal that he supposed to be not less than 90 feet in length. Mr. Davis doesn't think he saw any part of the body, but is positive it must've been not less than 40 feet in length, judging by the wake it left in the rear. It was going south, and all agreed that it swam with a speed almost incredible to their senses. Mr. Davis says he never saw a locomotive travel faster, and thinks it made a mile a minute easily. In a few minutes

after the discovery of the first, a second one followed in its wake; but it seemed to be much smaller, appearing to Mr. Slight about the size of a horse. A larger one, and all, and six small ones [went] southward out of sight.

One of the large ones, before disappearing, made a sudden turn to the west, a short distance; then back to its former track. At this turn Mr. Slight says he could distinctly see it was a brownish color. They could judge somewhat of their speed by observing known distances on the other side of the lake, and all agreed that the velocity with which they propelled themselves through the water was astonishing. They represent the waves that rolled up in front and on each side of them as being three feet high from where they stood. Messrs. Davis and Slight are prominent men, well known in this country, and all of them are reliable persons whose veracity is undoubted.

A giant prehistoric beaver could not reach a size of 90 feet, of course. But, perhaps Davis was mistaking the waves left in the creature's wake for a part of its body?

In 1870, a giant skull was found with large teeth that one could argue resembled a beaver's.

Springville, Sept. 7, 1870.
Editor Desert News:—Dear brother, the Messrs Dallin of this place, well known for their fishing proclivities, while plying their favorite vocation on the shores of the lake, found a section of the

ICE AGE

skull of the Lake Monster, at least all who have examined it, thus far, so suppose it.

The portion of the skull remaining is the left upper jaw. The teeth, judging from the apertures, must have been as large as those of an ox. It has a tusk projecting from the back teeth, five inches long; on the whole it is quite a curiosity.

The skull is in my possession and can be seen at any time.

Yours,

C. D. Evans.

As always, the skull was lost, never to be seen again.

Then, on July 19, 1871, two witnesses saw the head of the monster which they described as a walrus without tusks. On May 15, 1874, the monster was seen by famous Mormon pioneer and wagon train captain, William Budge. With Budge were two other witnesses, William Broomhead and Molando Pratt, to corroborate the sighting.

The sighting made such an impression on Budge he wrote a letter to Brigham Young himself. "At first sight we thought it might be a very large duck," he wrote to Young. Budge went on to write that he watched the creature swim in the waters of the lake about 20 yards from the shore. They estimated the animal to be about six feet long.

The creature dove under the water and then resurfaced, giving the men an even better look at it. Budge wrote, "It's face and part of its head was distinctly seen, covered with fur, or short hair of a light snuff color. The face of the animal was apparently flat, very wide between the eyes, and tapering to the nose with very full large eyes, and prominent ears, the ears resembling those of a horse, but scarcely as long. The whole face, in shape, was like that of a fox, but so large that the space between the eyes, equaled that of the distance between the eyes of a common cow."

WILLIAM L. BUDGE.

The monster was seen off and on for many years, and in the mid-1870s, Brigham Young even helped finance an effort to capture the beast. It was unsuccessful, naturally.

As stated earlier in this chapter, many Bear Lake monster sightings describe the creature as both reptilian and mammalian at different times. The below article should be of interest because it describes it as both at the same time! I've emboldened the contradictory aspects.

The Utah Lake Monster

According to the *Provo Inquirer*, the Utah Lake monster has been seen again recently, and that paper gives the following particulars:

The boys we allude to are named respectively, William Roberts and George Scott, and are known to be truthful and intelligent lads. They were bathing in the lake on Thursday last and had swam out some distance when they noticed something approaching **which they at first took for a dog and afterwards a beaver.** They went on swimming without noticing the animal again until a noise like the roar of a lion drew their attention once more to the object, and then they saw it still, traveling forwards and evidently approaching them – occasionally rising itself out of the water and showing its fore legs which were as long as a man's arm. The head of the animal as far as the boys were able to judge at that distance, which was about 20 or 30 yards, was from 2 to 3 feet long, and its mouth once open appeared to be about 18 inches wide. **The boys thought the mouth resembled that of an alligator as seen in picture books.**

As soon as the boys realized that the creature was making directly for them, and being alarmed by its loud roaring and savage gestures, they turned and swam towards the shore with all possible speed. As soon as they gained the shore then again looked at the animal and saw that it had gained on them, – in fact was but a few yards from the shore. It is needless to say that the little fellows "made tracks" for home without waiting to see if the creature could travel as well on land is by sea.

We will hear observed that the parents firmly believe the statements of the boys, who we are informed, look so terror-stricken as to make the neighbors believe that if they had not seen a monster, they must have seen something else equally as terrible.

The Bear Lake Monster, in its varying forms, continues to be seen to this day. But, like all lake monsters, its existence is still unproven.

"SNAIK STORIES"
THE FROZEN SEA SERPENT

☞ I INITIALLY COVERED the Ohio River Monster in the first *Cowboys & Saurians* book. The monster was sighted throughout the late 1800s and naturally caused quite a stir in both the Ohio and Mississippi Rivers. This "cold case" may, in fact, detail one of the monster's additional adventures, and possibly its final icy fate...

From the *Terre Haute Daily Wabash Express* on January 23, 1883:

THE RIVER MONSTER
Seen For the First Time in Years at Rose Clare, Ills., Last Sunday.

Evansville Courier.
For several years, at intervals of time, we have heard brief accounts of the appearance, at different points, of a huge marine monster in the form of a snake, making its appearance at divers places in the Mississippi and Ohio valleys. The accounts have ever been of an indefinite character and colored with such exaggeration as would bear away all semblance of truth into the realm of mystical fiction. The account which is here given of the latest appearance of his snakeship is vouched for by more than a dozen eye witnesses, and we should refrain from this lengthy preface, but for fear of

our account being misconstrued into one of the common canards for the purpose of a sensation.

On Sunday morning last, as two boatmen were endeavoring to extricate a flat boat, which had been caught in the ice just below Rose Clare, Ills., they were startled by a peculiar hissing, whistling noise in close proximity to their boat. Each looked in the direction and saw a writhing, twisted form, apparently issuing from between two great blocks of ice. It was soon evident that the sea serpent (for such it was) had become fastened between the boulders of ice, and was floundering with terrific force and violence to extricate itself. Fully twenty feet of the forepart of its body was above the water, while its extremity was occasionally revealed, afar downstream, apparently encircling the great block of ice and exhibiting a visible length of more than one hundred feet. It had evidently become caught while coming from beneath the ice, and was now struggling in all the throes of great agony and madness. It would raise its head as high as possible, and extending its great jaws would dash against either piece of ice with all the force of an immense living sledge hammer. At one time it grasped the block in its teeth, and with mastodon strength tore away a fragment of several tons, lifting it high in the air and dashed it to atoms. This would have relieved it from the perilous position, but the part of its body which had been wedged in seemed to have become numbed and lifeless, and the monster made all sorts of gyrations, trying to draw himself upward.

ICE AGE

Realizing its helpless condition, a stroke of human reasoning seemed to possess it. Darting its head quickly beneath the ice pack, it actually came up in a moment with the nether part of its body between its teeth. All this while the two boatmen and serpent had continued to float downstream, and, in the meantime, the strange sight had been witnessed by other parties along the shore, who ran and spread the news to neighbors, and in a brief while all the denizens of that locality were lining the river bank and stretching their optics for a clearer view of this almost fabulous dragon.

The serpent seemed suddenly to fall into a sort of torpor as soon as he had gotten clearly upon the ice-float and coiled himself into one immense jumble, which no doubt aided in restoring his vitality, by thus warming his benumbed form. A rifle shot fired by one of the party on the shore aroused him from his icy siesta, and with a sudden plunge he disappeared beneath the ice and was seen to rise but once, about midway the river, as he seemed swimming for the opposite shore, since which time has been seen no more.

This strange marine animal has, as we said before, made its appearance at two or three different times in the past—once near Quincy, Ills., in the Mississippi, and another time near Vicksburg, Miss., near the mouth of Red River. One of the most singular things being his almost miraculous disappearance, and being seen no more in the same locality. The impression prevails that it buries itself in the mud at the bottom of the river, and is capable of remaining in this condition for months at a time. How it lives, on what it subsists and its strange nature is left for the future to solve.

3
IDAHO BILL AND THE SABERTOOTH TIGER
MYSTERY BEAST FROM MEXICO

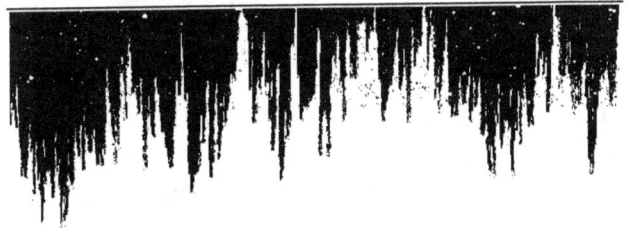

IN TERMS OF POPULARITY where Ice Age animals are concerned, the sabertooth tiger easily comes in at second place behind the mammoth. And while there have been plenty of mammoth sightings in the realm of cryptozoology, sightings of saber-toothed tigers are scarce by comparison.

In the Western Hemisphere, the highest density of sightings seems to come from—of all places—Mexico and the Southwest. Mexico, in particular, has legends of the *onza*, a feline cryptid with varying descriptions. Notably, in 1994, a saber-toothed cat was spotted in Northern Mexico by Roberto Guitierrez, according to an article in an issue of *Science Ilustrée* in 1998. To the north, in New Mexico, a man named Jerry Padilla claimed that a late relative of his had seen one on a mountain road in the northern part of the state in 1946.

The most interesting story concerning a sabertooth tiger came courtesy of Karl Shuker's *Still in Search of Prehistoric Survivors*. Shuker writes, "In June 2016, Richard Muirhead sent me a series of newspaper articles concerning a mysterious, unidentified animal that he speculates may have been a living sabre-tooth from Mexico."[15]

The article ran in the August 2, 1928 issue of the *Morning Oregonian*, and as I cannot find the original article, I shall use Shuker's reproduction as my reference. The story tells of a Wild West showman named Colonel Barney "Idaho Bill" Pearson rolling up to the offices of the *Morning Oregonian* with a strange animal in the back of his truck.

Shuker's reproduction of the article is as follows:

> ...[Pearson] declared he had an animal, which has yet received no name— either as a scientific identification or as a family name such as pets often have— hidden away in that cage. Tarpaulins, rags, sheets of tin, close screen netting and what-nots entirely covered the cage, and so the crowd was not allowed to see enough to satisfy its curiosity. Two lucky newspapermen were the only ones allowed to peek in, and they'll tell the world there was a Whatizis in there because it growled at both of them at once.

---

[15] Shuker, *Still in Search of Prehistoric Survivors*, pp.455.

ICE AGE

Beast Comes From Mexico

The beast was captured in Mexico southwest of Mexico City about three months ago, the colonel explained, and he is now taking it east to Washington, D.C., where it will be given a scientific identification. So far the colonel does not know what it is that rides with him.

Anyway, it weighs 800 pounds, looks like a combination of tiger, lion and cougar; growls like all of them together; has claws like a cat, has stripes like a tiger, a square snout, shaggy hair around its shoulders and tusks in its mouth.

"What does it eat?" an onlooker queried.

"One calf every 2 ½ days," the colonel replied. "When I can't get a calf I have to buy fresh meat from a butcher shop. That's why I look so disreputable myself."

Going east from Portland the colonel expects to "percolate" over the Columbia Highway to Pendleton and over the Old Oregon Trail to Yellowstone Park and thence on eastward to Washington.[16]

I was able to find the follow-up article, as printed in the *Ogden Standard Examiner,* on August 18, 1928. In full, it reads:

---

[16] Ibid.

COWBOYS & SAURIANS

HUGE WILDCAT ENROUTE EAST
"Indian Bill" Ropes Animal Which He Can't Classify

TWIN FALLS, Aug. 18—(AP)—Colonel B.R. Pearson, widely known as "Idaho Bill," scout, guide and outstanding figure of the frontier west arrived here Friday night by automobile with a monster cat as passenger.

Colonel Pearson is en route to Washington to present the beast to the National zoological society. The animal is about twice as large as a mountain lion, with peculiar beard and markings similar to those of a tiger. Its ears resemble those of a gorilla. The colonel expects the animal, which he captured in southern Mexico, will be identified at the zoological gardens.

Six men assisted Mr. Pearson in roping the beast in its native haunts, where it was believed to have killed several humans. One of the assistants was severely injured by the big cat, and a second victim, the colonel said, was a spectator who thought the animal a "show animal" and moved too close to the cage. His face was laid open with a sweep of the cat's paw.

On the trip east, Colonel Pearson is traveling only during the daytime, in order, he said, to avoid risk of mishap which might result in liberation of his "pet." A young calf fed to the animal every two and one-half days is constituting its rations on the trip.

ICE AGE

Colonel Pearson recalled last night that he first had traversed the Snake river valley of southern Idaho with his father, a California pioneer of 1840, in 1872. Thirty years ago, he said, he was engaged in "running wild cattle and wild horses" through this valley as an employee of J. H. Burks. At American Falls he said he became adept at crossing brands of cattle and horses.

Since that time, Mr. Pearson said, he has visited in turn Alaska, Africa and Central America and has served as companion and guide on many hunting expeditions including some of those made by the late Colonel Theodore Roosevelt.

And did "Idaho Bill" make it to Washington, D.C., with his prehistoric prize? Of course, the answer is no—or at least not that we know of. Shuker reports that he was given a newspaper article dated November 28, 1930, from the *Council Bluffs Nonpareil*. It revealed that three weeks earlier, Pearson's truck became overturned in an accident, and the animal escaped. That's not the only problem. Pearson didn't describe the animal as feline-like. He said it resembled a gorilla, called it his pet, and furthermore claimed that it was not dangerous. Considering that this article takes place two whole years since the previous article, I would like to instead speculate that perhaps this was an entirely different animal altogether? After all, surely it wouldn't take the man two whole years to get to Washington, D.C.?

IDAHO BILL.

Though I can't confirm that "Idaho Bill" ever captured a bonafide sabertoothed tiger (or a Sasquatch), I can at least confirm that he was real. Idaho Bill was the subject of many write-ups before and after the monster cat story, and the details presented in the articles are both encouraging and discouraging at the same time. As to discouraging aspects, Idaho Bill was quite the showman and attention seeker. Like many western stars of the time, he claimed to not remember how old he actually was, nor how many cattle he owned. Naturally, he had ridden with the James Boys, Billy the Kid, and Buffalo Bill Cody in his younger days. This is troubling because this same behavior was exhibited by men such as Brushy Bill Roberts, who, for example, claimed to be Billy the Kid, rode with Buffalo Bill Cody, and could not remember exactly how old he was.

As to facts I learned that corroborated details in the "monster cat" story, numerous articles stated that Pearson made many trips into Mexico. He also had a penchant for capturing dangerous animals. On December 12, 1923, on page seven of the *Logansport Morning Press*, the following story told of how he delivered wild animals to the White House.

Grizzly Bears For President

"Idaho Bill" Pearson Delivers Gift in Dodge Car

R B. Pearson, "Colonel Idaho Bill," rolled into the White House a week ago to present President Coolidge with a brace of wild bears. He had them with him, outside in a dodge Brothers screen sidecar.

"Colonel Bill" has long made his home in the West, moving further and further into the wilds as settlement has forced him from the mountains of Mexico, where he captured the bears that he gave to the President.

COWBOYS & SAURIANS

President Coolidge enjoyed the presentation ceremony immensely. Known as a man who seldom smiles, he enjoyed the antics of the bears with all of the enthusiasm of a school boy.

There is no doubt about the bears being wild. They carry numerous marks of combat with horses and cattle in the wilds of Mexico. Their spirit has in no way been subdued by their motor trip across the country. They will be turned over to the National Zoological Park.

Claud Zook, of Zook Bros., local representatives, says: "The Dodge Brothers car used in delivering the bears made 4,000 miles on this particular trip from Mexico and has made a total of 100,000 miles in exploration and hunting trips undertaken by the Colonel. And these trips have been in the wildest and the roughest parts of the United States and Mexico.

This article is encouraging for a number of reasons. First, Pearson was reputable enough to gain an audience with the president. Second, this established that he was familiar with capturing dangerous animals in Mexico. Third, it also showed that he had a relationship with the National Zoological Park, which he intended to give his monster cat to.

In 1940, potential physical evidence of surviving saber-tooth tigers in Mexico was unearthed by none other than Ivan T. Sanderson. That year he was given the skin of a mysterious big cat from Mexico, which natives said had been killed recently. It measured 6 feet long and had both dark and light brown stripes across it. Oddest of all was a hairy tuft that grew in between the shoulders, neck, and ears. Sanderson called it the "Mexican Ruffed Cat," but other cryptozoologists speculated that it could be a saber-toothed tiger.

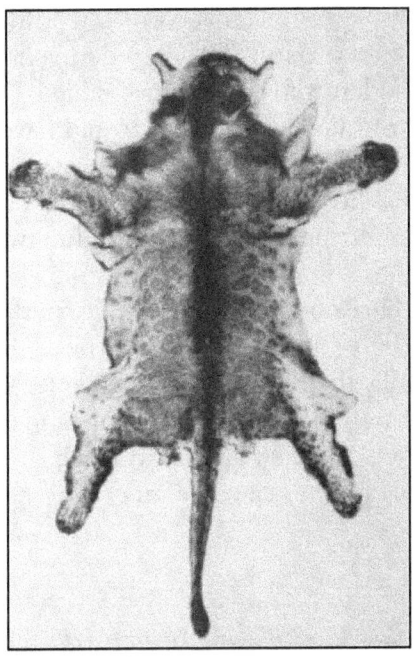

**PELT OF AFRICAN
MYSTERY CAT C. 1931.**

And where is this potential evidence today? Sadly, Sanderson had bad luck when it came to proof of mysterious creatures. It was Sanderson who claimed to have a copy of the notorious Thunderbird photo that purported to show a huge, bird-like animal killed by cowboys in Tombstone, Arizona, in the late 1880s. He loaned it out to some fellow researchers who never returned it. Likewise, the skin of the "Mexican Ruffed Cat" was destroyed when the building housing it flooded.[17]

And what of old Colonel Pearson? He died in 1942 at the age of 74 in Hollywood, California, where he was helping in the production of Western movies. If the age given is correct, that means that Pearson was born in 1868. Considering he claimed to have ridden with Jesse James (killed 1882) and Billy the Kid (killed 1881), he would have to have been riding with the notorious outlaws in his very early teens. Possible, but still a bit unlikely (unless he was referring to riding with the two men's posthumous doppelgangers, J. Frank Dalton and Brushy Bill Roberts. Roberts was a performer in Buffalo Bill's Circus, so in all fairness, that could be the "Billy the Kid" he was referring to).

In closing, there is substantial evidence that Pearson was a skilled animal wrangler, it's just not certain that he ever caught a sabertooth tiger.

Sources:

Shuker, Karl. *Still In Search of Prehistoric Survivors*. Greeneville, OH: Coachwhip Publications, 2016.

Swancer, "Mysterious Encounters with Supposedly Extinct Ice Age Monsters," Mysterious Universe.org. https://mysteriousuniverse.org/2018/01/mysterious-encounters-with-supposedly-extinct-ice-age-monsters/

---

[17] Swancer, "Mysterious Encounters," MysteriousUniverse.org.

"SNAIK STORIES"
MONSTER OF THE MINE

☞ ON MY OWN, I found only one North American sabertooth tiger sighting. It was recounted by a man from Idaho in 1922, though the story itself takes place in Larimer County, Colorado. It's enough to make me wonder if Colonel Pearson heard this story back in 1922. Here is the relevant portion of the article, "Waverlyite Unbeatable Telling Fish Stories," as presented in the *Fort Collins Courier* on January 11, 1922:

Strange things, too, happen at the Tenny coal mine where Ben Widman and Johnson are taking our coal. From what we can learn, through Arthur Hess and young Weyman, there is a strange animal hidden away in the dark recesses of this renowned coal mine. A description of the creature reads like a sketch from Ben Widman's fervid imagination or a page from Prof. Osborn's "Men of the Old Stone Age," wherein he describes the long extinct "saber tooth tiger." Some little while ago these young men, in a dark and unused portion of the mine, sighted the strange animal. They lost no time in seeking light and safety. From what we can learn they came out of the mine, bumping against props, supports, etc. "Almost," Jim Rogers would say, "as if the devil were after them." Others too, report seeing and hearing strange things down in this mine. In the tiger theory we take little stock. The only tiger known to the Waverlyites is the one known as "Blind" and if such a one were known to be "at large" in the mine neighborhood, the mines would immediately become the most popular place in Larimer county.

DEPICTION OF SABERTOOTH TIGER, C.LATE 1800s.

4
PRAIRIE DOG MONSTER OF NEMAHA COUNTY
A GLYPTODONT IN NEBRASKA?

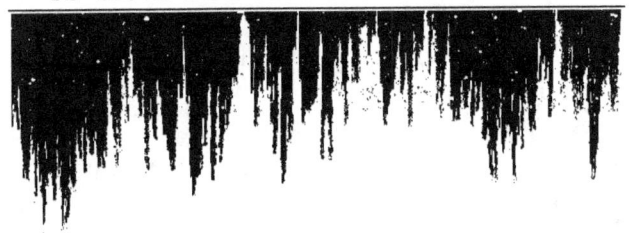

WHEN RIFLING THROUGH old newspapers one will usually find very interesting—and unfortunately very short—blurbs on some sort of creature or phenomenon. Usually, these blurbs lack much detail and offer only a few tantalizing lines of information. Said stories are also usually never followed up upon. A great example of this is this little nugget from the *Beatrice Daily Sun* from October 22, 1904, which reports that:

Over in Nemaha county [Nebraska] people are all worked up over the appearance of an animal that seems to be a cross between a dinosaur and a ground hog. Some people think that the strange beast is the sea serpent that has come up the river from its ocean home.

A cross between "a dinosaur and a groundhog", what on earth could match such a description? When I mentioned the strange creature to a friend in passing, they joked that maybe "they just saw a big armadillo."

Ironically enough, a prehistoric armadillo called the glyptodont might be the closest thing to a "dinosaur crossed with a groundhog." The heavily armored glyptodont was around 13 feet long and lived up until the Pleistocene.

Whether the residents of Nemaha County were seeing a live glyptodont or not, the creatures were rumored to still be living in South America at one time. In the 19th Century, people in Brazil and Uruguay began hearing strange underground noises. Soon after, they started noticing large furrows and tunnels in the ground near rivers and lakes. These tunnels were so large that they would occasionally alter the course of rivers. Hillsides too would sometimes collapse, and even portions of an apple orchard fell into the ground. But that wasn't the worst of it. Suddenly, horses and other livestock crossing the Rio dos Piloes would suddenly be pulled under by a mysterious animal, dubbed the Minhocão.

Some eyewitness sightings of the Minhocão seem similar to a glyptodont. A dead specimen was allegedly seen by a man named Lebino Jose dos Santos in Uruguay in 1849. The creature had died when it had become stuck in between two rock

ICE AGE

clefts and couldn't get out. Santos described its skin as being "as thick as the bark of a pine tree, and formed of hard scales like those of an armadillo."[18]

**DOEDICURUS AND GLYPTODONT
BY ROBERT BRUCE HORSFALL C.1912.**

A sighting in 1870 in Lages, Brazil, told of Francisco de Amaral Varella sighting "a strange animal of gigantic size" on the bank of the Rio das Caveiras. Varella said that the creature was "nearly one meter in thickness, not very long, and with the snout like a pig."[19]

These are but a few stories and sightings of the glyptodont-like Minhocão in South America. Considering that the people of Nemaha County considered their monster to be a cross between a groundhog (a burrowing animal like the Minhocão)

---

[18] Shuker, *Prehistoric Survivors*, pp.146.
[19] Ibid.

and a dinosaur, a glyptodont would seem to be the best candidate. What's more interesting is the exact wording of the article where it says, "Some people think that the strange beast is *the* sea serpent that has come up the river from its ocean home." Because it says 'the' sea serpent rather than 'a' sea serpent, one might assume that a monster had been sighted previously in a nearby river?[20] Couple this with the fact that the Minhocão spent time in the water and perhaps that's what the monster of Nemaha County really was?

Sources:

Shuker, Karl. *In Search of Prehistoric Survivors: Do Giant Extinct Creatures Still Exist?* London: Blandford, 1995.

---

[20] I could find no mention of sea serpent or river monster sightings reported previously in the area.

5
BACK TO THE STONE AGE
NEVADA'S NEO CAVEMAN

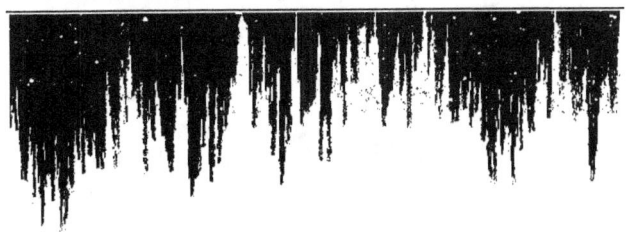

IT IS THOUGHT THAT during the Ice Age that modern homo sapiens, or "cavemen," lived side by side with some remnant Neanderthals. There are even a few who think that some of the more humanoid Bigfoot sightings are in fact surviving Neanderthals.

During the Pioneer Period, any man-like entity glimpsed in nature was often referred to as a "wild man." Therefore, back then, the term "wild man" could refer to a wide variety of beings. Many wild men were just that, men who had abandoned society to live in the wilderness with wild, unkempt hair. A few even dressed in loincloths like Tarzan. Then there were the really hairy ones, which we would now recognize as Bigfoot or Sasquatch. But again, back then, a "wild man" was simply a "wild man"—be it human or hominid.

Our next story occurred in the vicinity of Deep Creek, Elko County, Nevada. The sighting took place in July of 1870 and was published in *The Public Ledger* out of Memphis, Tennessee, on July 26, 1870. The story details what is either a bonafide caveman that survived into the modern day, or simply a modern-day man who decided to revert to the simpler ways of his ancestors.

> The people inhabiting the northwestern part of Nevada are at present in an intense state of excitement over the supposed discovery of the traces and habitation of a lost or wild man. Rumor had located it upon a high and densely wooded mountain, and after gathering all the information that we could, we armed and equipped ourselves for a trip to the location described, about fifty miles from our camp, at the sink of Deep Creek.
>
> After a tiresome ride of two days over the mountain, all were now upon the *qui vive*[21] for some sign of the strange inhabitant. We had just picketed our animals, and sat by the fire telling strange experiences of the pioneer life, when we were aroused by a crashing sound, caused by the swift approach of some strange looking body coming toward the camp. Just at this moment, the moon shone through the clouds almost as brilliant as the sun at noon-day.

---

[21] An old slang term for "on the lookout."

ICE AGE

We had a splendid view of the object. It is undoubtedly a white man, about forty years old, nearly covered by a coat of fine long hair, and in appearance otherwise not at all startling. He carried in his right hand a huge club, and in his left a rabbit or some other small animal. He caught sight of us almost instantaneously, as the moon shone out, and with a scream like the roar of a lion, brandishing his club, dashed past the camp and attacked the horses in a perfect frenzy of madness.

We at this time could have shot him but for the surprise of the moment; and [though] we were armed, our animals stampeded and he was after them like the wind, down the mountain. We endeavored in vain to send our dogs after him, which, being savage and well trained, we had counted upon to assist in the capture; but with distended eyes they sat mutely gazing into the darkness, and neither blows nor kindness could move them to the chase, and the only recourse we had was to throw up a rampart of logs and then station guards to prevent a surprise by the infuriated demon.

Occasionally, through the long watches of the night, all hands were aroused by his terrible cries; and thus, in momentary expectation of an attack, we passed the night. Morning dawned at last, and not one would leave the camp until the rosy sunlight cheered the landscape, which we took the trail of our horses, after having securely hidden our accouterments and provisions, excepting a lunch for a few days journey. They had torn down the mountain at a terrific speed for about five miles; here they jumped down a sheer precipice about twenty five feet, disabling my saddle horse. He was lying near the bottom, mangled in a shocking manner.

The wild man had evidently vented his rage upon my disabled horse, as large strips of skin were torn off and thrown to some distance, and his lower jaw was broken. We shot him to end his sufferings. The wild man had here given up the pursuit. About two miles further down the valley we found the rest of our stock quietly grazing. The only marks they bore were

ICE AGE

evidently made by being caught by the tails by the wild man in the chase, entirely stripping some of them of their hair and skin.

We now had some six miles to go to reach our first camp. Arrived there at 3 o'clock, when we took lunch. After examining our arms, we started in the direction from which the wild man approached and was fortunate enough to strike his trail, with the well-defined footprints of a man who would wear No. 9 shoes, but being broad on the bottom. We followed his trail for about three minutes, when the gorges opened in a beautiful basin, and a half mile further the trail ended abruptly at the entrance of a cave.

We explored this cave, finding a set of soldier's buttons and a dime dated 1841, which leads me to the conclusion that he is a man lost from Fremont's command in 1846 or near that time.

This article's conclusion seems to wrap up the mystery of the wildman in a rather tidy bow. Given the year the story was set in, that being 1870, and that the witnesses estimated him to be a man in his 40s, then it seems entirely likely he was a soldier who decided to live out the rest of his days in the wild. The man was also quite mad, which would account for the howling and so forth (or, the article's writer just wanted to color his account of the wildman a bit).

However, though men can get quite hairy whilst living ungroomed in the wild, the witnesses described this wildman as "nearly covered by a coat of fine long hair." The fact that he tore patches of skin from the horses was also a bit disturbing, though his nails were probably quite sharp from living in such an unkempt manner for so long.

Whether the man had been a humanoid Sasquatch, a surviving Neanderthal, or merely an ex-soldier, he was most certainly a "caveman."

Sources:

Rosales, Albert S. *Humanoid Encounters: 1 A.D.-1899: The Others Amongst Us.* Triangulum Publishing, 2017.

6
SOUTHERN SARKASTODON OF GEORGIA
OXYAENIDAE ON THE LOOSE?

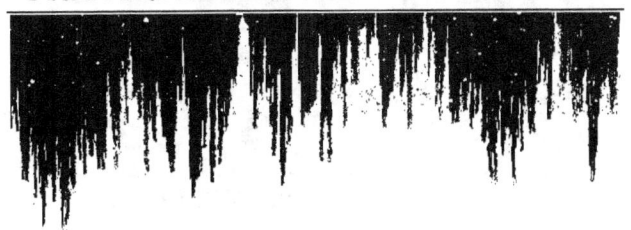

IF YOU WERE TO FAKE a sighting of an Ice Age creature, what variety would you choose? Chances are that you'd pick something commonly known: a mammoth, a sabertooth tiger, or maybe even a giant sloth. But would you pick something as obscure as a Sarkastodon?

The Sarkastodon was a large Ice Age mammal that looked like a huge bear with a long tail like a feline's. It was about ten feet long (not counting the tail), and when on all fours, about six feet tall. The Sarkastodon was a member of the Oxyaenidae family. These carnivorous mammals were often cat-like and sometimes had hyena-like jaws.

COWBOYS & SAURIANS

RESTORATION OF PATRIOFELIS, A SPECIES OF OXYAENIDAE, BY CHARLES KNIGHT.

In the year 1897, chances are you would not know what a Sarkastodon was, because the animal's fossils weren't discovered until 1930 all the way over in Mongolia. In February of 1897, a man living in Fletcherville, Georgia, saw what could have very well been a Sarkastodon that was not yet fully grown. The article was published in the February 13, 1897 issue of the *Thomasville Times Enterprise*, and won't be reprinted in full because, quite frankly, it is very derogatory to African Americans at times:

The Story of a Strange Animal.

The [African American population] in the town is muchly wrought up over a strange animal which is said to be prowling about Fletcherville and beyond, after the shades of night have gathered. Those who have seen it—or say they have seen it—aver that it is something like a bear, with a great long tail. As the story goes, it has killed and maimed a number of dogs—and this reminds us that this is a blessing, though it may be in disguise, as there are many surplus dogs, of low degree infesting that and other portions of the town. It is also said that it killed a fine fat calf the other night. Part of the calf was found... Both the hind-quarters were missing. This is, to say the least of it, rather a suspicious circumstance. Has some impecunious [African American] been feasting on these missing hindquarters?

In only one instance, it seems, has this strange animal come into direct contact with anyone. A few nights ago a colored waiter at one of the hotels, whose wages enable him to sport a beaver hat and carry an umbrella, was out calling on his dulcena. Oblivious of his immediate surroundings, forgetful of broken crockery and exacting guests, he was swinging along at a lively gait, when, all at once, the strange animal confronted him. The capillary substance fairly raised his shining beaver, while a cold sweat began oozing from the pores of his skin. With a whack of his umbrella, he jumped backwards and gave a yell which would have discounted the screech of a Comanche Indian. And they do say that the ground thereabouts was badly torn up when seen next morning.

Every [African American] in town religiously believes that the strange animal is around. While this belief lasts—and pity that it will soon be dissipated—chickens can roost on the lower limbs with perfect impunity.

The Story of this strange animal would be incomplete without the statement that it is not known what brand of liquor the victim of the broken umbrella uses; though it is presumably bad.

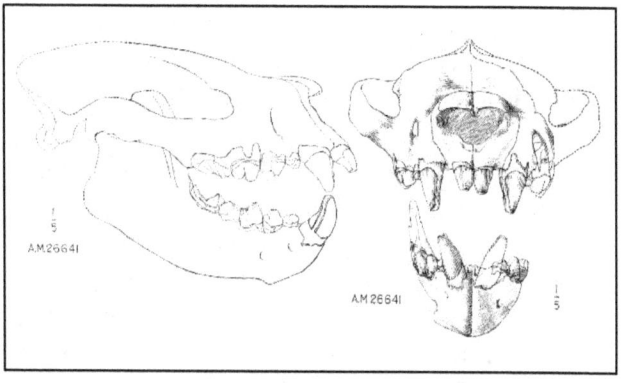

ILLUSTRATION OF A SARKASTODON SKULL FROM A 1938 REPORT.

If this article was simply made up to poke fun at Fletcherville's African American population is unknown, but the description of "something like a bear, with a great long tail" is eyebrow-raising. It was also not the only sighting of such a creature.

Four years earlier, a similar creature was sighted near Atlanta. The *Atlanta Constitution* published the following account on March 18, 1893:

ICE AGE

Mysterious Dog-Killer

A mysterious animal attacked and killed dogs in the Atlanta suburb of West End in the first weeks of March. Over a three-day period, no fewer than six were slain, two of them mostly devoured. On three occasions, each of them at dusk, witnesses saw, or thought they saw, the killer, and twice it was fired upon, without apparent effect.

One witness said its outline was that of an enormous bear. Another said the creature looked like a large Newfoundland dog. A third swore it was a hyena.

The creature would come out of a woods located near a cemetery. Local people were terrified, and some refused to leave their houses after dark. Hunting parties trying to run down the strange beast were invariably unsuccessful.

Again, the key in the description here is the comparison between a bear and hyena. Considering that they took place in the same state, this could have been the same creature, or, if nothing else, the same species.

Nearly 30 years later, in Arizona, another possible Sarkastodon was sighted in the vicinity of the Huachuca Mountains (the same area where the Tombstone Thunderbird was sighted in 1890).

On February 11, 1924, the *Miami Daily Arizona Silver Belt* reported that "a strange species of animal appearing to be a cross between a bear and a lion has made its appearance in the Huachucas..."

The article goes on to report how an "old time pioneer" shot the animal when it attacked his dog.

The man, J.H. Merritt, said, "I have his hide here. He is built like a bear and has a foot like one, but has a tail as long as a lion's and I never saw such tusks as he had."

And now onto a rather important question: are there any Sarkastodon-like cryptids sighted today? The answer is yes, but all the way over in China. The creature is called the Guoshanhuang and is seen in the Shennonjia Forestry District and Huping Mountains. Though often described as something more akin to a saber-toothed tiger, a few witnesses have described an animal more in line with a Sarkastodon. Supposedly one was even shot and killed in 1975, though, naturally, the remains have never been made public.

In North America, Cryptozoologist David Weatherly has found a few reports of extraordinarily large bears in the Four Corners area of the Southwest, which he thinks could be a Sarkastodon. One farmer saw a "bear as big as a horse" in one instance.[22]

So, though rare, there are other instances of what could be remnant Sarkastodons sighted today. If that's what was sighted in Fletcherville is anyone's guess—and at the moment, the Sarkastodon is the best guess for me.

---

[22] https://cryptomundo.com/cryptozoologists/cave-bear-cryptid-canines-more/

ICE AGE

Sources:

Cox, Barry and Colin Harrison. *The Simon & Schuster Encyclopedia of Dinosaurs & Prehistoric Creatures.* New York, NY: Simon & Schuster, 1999.

Prothero, Donald R. *The Princeton Field Guide to Prehistoric Mammals.* Princeton, NJ: Princeton University Press, 2017.

Weatherly, David. "Cave Bear, Crytpid Canines and More." Cryptomundo. (October 14th, 2013)
https://cryptomundo.com/cryptozoologists/cave-bear-cryptid-canines-more/

"NOT A PLEASANT LOOKING CUSTOMER."

☞ THE FOLLOWING was published in the December 31, 1884 *Fort Wayne Daily Gazette*. It is one of many mystery animals in this book to be confused for a bear, a large feline, and a hyena to name a few:

"Ohio State News"

A strange wild animal has been creating consternation in the vicinity of Glenford. The beast has been called a panther, a lynx, a hyena, a bear and dear knows what other names. Several efforts have been made to bring it down with a gun, but without effect. What it is or where it came from are both alike unknown. The beast is not a pleasant looking customer. A combined effort will probably be made to dispatch the roaming animal.

7
MAMMOTHS ALIVE
MASTODONS IN ALASKA

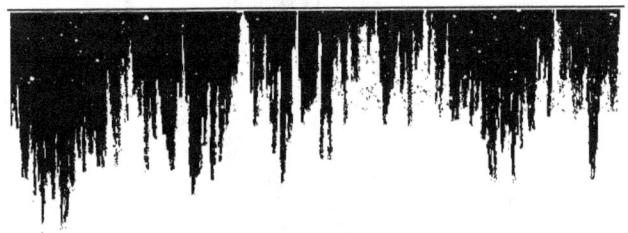

OF ALL THE ICE AGE creatures, the mammoth is easily the best known. It was slightly larger—and definitely hairier—than today's African elephant. It lived during the Pleistocene epoch, and some theorize it survived past that and only went extinct 4,000 years ago. From time to time, frozen specimens have been found in Alaska and Siberia and are not uncommon. The first was found as far back as 1692. The best known, a baby mammoth nicknamed "Dima," was discovered in Siberia in 1977.

In Alaska, in the late 1880s, an old fur trapper traded some natives for a pair of enormous ivory tusks said to have come from a mammoth. That, in of itself, was not strange. As already stated, finding a frozen mammoth wasn't impossible. What alarmed the fur trader was that the tusks contained traces of fresh blood!

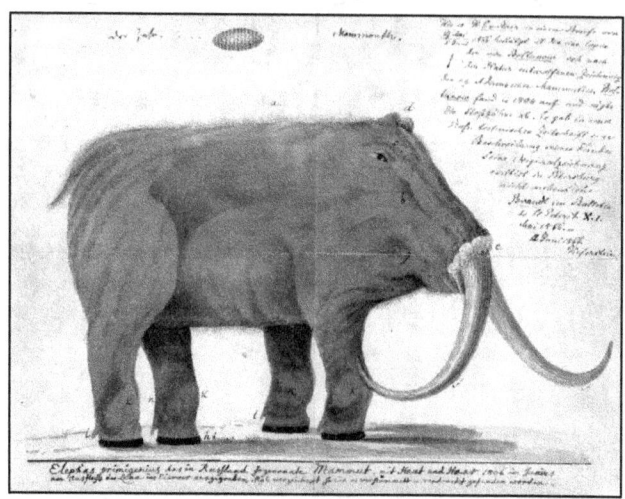

EARLY DAY INTERPRETATION OF MAMMOTH CARCASS C.1800.

An article on the incredible story was published in the *Wichita Eagle* out of Kansas on July 26, 1889:

VALUABLE DISCOVERY MADE BY THE ALASKA FUR COMPANY.

Monster Creatures Twenty Feet High and Thirty Feet in Length - Tusks Weighing 250 Pounds - Garden "Sass" and Glaciers Side by Side.

"Alaska is a country of paradoxes!"

ICE AGE

That is what Mr. Cola F. Fowler, of the Alaska Fur and Commercial company, said in answer to the question of a reporter respecting his late field of operations.

"During all that time, up to two months ago, when I resigned and started for home," said Mr. Fowler, "I have had my headquarters at Kodiac, which is the most northern station occupied by agents of our company. We have our headquarters in San Francisco, and trading stations all over Secretary Seward's purchase. As yet Alaska is almost a terra incognita. The country immediately surrounding some of the principal rivers like the Yukon, Snake and Stickeer has been explored, and a few miles inland from the coast line, but the great interior is almost unknown. What we have learned of it is a surprise, and was the foundation of my answer to your question.

"Alaska is certainly a country of paradoxes. You who live here in the states look upon it as a land of perpetual ice and snow, and yet you would be astonished if I told you that I grew in my garden at Kodiac abundant crops of radishes, lettuce, carrots, onions, cauliflowers, cabbage, peas, turnips, potatoes, beets, parsnips and celery. Within five miles of this garden was one of the largest glaciers in Alaska, and between the fertile coast slip and the interior is reared along the entire sea boundary a continuous mountain of perpetual ice and snow.

"During your twelve years' residence in Alaska what was the most wonderful thing you ever saw or heard there?"

Mr. Fowler smiled at this question, and, after a moment's hesitation said: "Two years ago last summer I left Kodiak for a trip to the headwaters of the Snake River, where our traveling agents had established a trading station at an Indian village. The chief of this family of Innuits was named To-lee-ti-ma, and to him I was recommended. He received me hospitably, and I at once began negotiations for the purchase of a big lot of fossil ivory which his tribe had cached near the village. The lot weighed several thousand pounds, and was composed of the principal and inferior tusks of the mammoth, the remains of thousands of which gigantic animals are to be found in the bed of interior Alaskan water courses. I subjected the ivory to a rigid inspection, and upon two of the largest tusks I discovered fresh blood traces and the remains of partly decomposed flesh.

"I questioned To-lee-ti-ma, and he assured me that less than three months before a party of his young men had encountered a drove of monsters about fifty miles above where he was then encamped, and he succeeded in killing two, an old bull and a cow. At my request he sent for the leader of the hunting party, a young and intelligent Indian, and I questioned him closely about his adventure among a race of animals that the scientific people claim are extinct. He told a straightforward story, and I have no reason to doubt its truth.

KILLING A MONSTER.

"He and his band were searching along a dry water course for ivory, and had found a considerable quantity. One of the bucks, who was in advance, rushed in upon the main body one morning with the startling intelligence that at a spring of water about a mile above where they then were he had discovered the 'sign' of several of the 'big teeth.' They had come down to the spring to drink from a lofty plateau farther inland, and had evidently fed in the vicinity of the water for some time. The chief immediately called about him his warriors, and the party, under the leadership of the scout, approached the stream.

"They had nearly reached it when their ears were suddenly saluted by a chorus of loud, shrill, trumpet like calls, and an enormous creature came crashing toward them through the thicket, the ground fairly trembling beneath its ponderous footfalls. With wild cries of terror and dismay the Indians fled, all but the chief and the scout who had first discovered the trail of the monsters. They were armed with large caliber muskets and stood their ground, opening fire on the mammoth. A bullet must have penetrated the creature's brain, for it staggered forward and fell dead, and subsequently, on their way back to their campground, they overhauled and killed a cow 'big teeth,' which was evidently the mate of the first one killed.

"I asked the hunter to describe the monster, and, taking a sharp stick, he drew me a picture of the male animal in the soft clay. According to his description it was at least twenty feet in height and thirty feet in length. In general shape it was not unlike an elephant, but its ears were smaller, its eyes bigger and its trunk longer and more slender. Its tusks were yellowish white in color and six in number. Four of these tusks were placed like those of a boar, one on either side in each jaw; they were about four feet long and came to a sharp point. The other two tusks he brought away.

"I measured them and they were over fifteen feet in length and weighed upwards of 250 pounds each. They gradually tapered to a sharp point and curved inward. The monster's body was covered with long, coarse hair of a reddish dun color. I took a copy of the rude sketch made by the Indian.

"By the way, our late governor, the Hon. Alfred P. Swineford, has pretty carefully investigated the matter, and he is certain from a thorough sifting of native testimony that large herds of these monsters are to be found on the high plateaus in interior Alaska about the headwaters of the Snake river."

- Philadelphia Press

In trying to find a record of Mr. Fowler, all I could dig up was a small mention in the book *Fur*

ICE AGE

Seal Arbitration published in 1895. It listed a Mr. Fowler as an "Agent of North American Commercial Company." If this is even the same Mr. Fowler, who can say? But the book concerned the northern regions of Alaska and Canada. I found mention of the same Mr. Fowler and the same company again in the *Seal and Salmon Fisheries and General Resources of Alaska, Volume 2* investigating a group of dead seal pups. Of course, proving that Fowler was real doesn't prove that his story was real, but it helps.

The descriptions of the mammoths given were spot on except for a few odd details. That these mammoths had six tusks does not line up with known discoveries at all. If we're to take this story seriously, we might have to assume that these men saw a heretofore undiscovered subspecies of mammoths with more than one pair of tusks.[23] On the other hand, the detail that the animal's ears were slightly smaller than modern elephants was spot on. The size of the tusks, over 15 feet, though large, is also accurate as tusks of that size have been discovered before. The size of the creatures, being 20 feet in height, is about five feet over the height of the biggest mammoth. However, another mammoth witness in Canada from years before had also described the creatures as 20 feet tall.

---

[23] To be thorough, baby mammoths have a preliminary set of tusks that fall out and are replaced by permanent tusks. In that sense one could argue mammoths have two pair of tusks, but not at the same time.

MAMMOTH BY CHARLES KNIGHT C.1909.

In 1803 near York Fort[24] in Western Canada, a sergeant in the Hudson Bay Company named Thomas Pollock came across a strange animal. Pollock wrote the following account of the animal, which was published years later in the *Scots Magazine* on Wednesday, July 1, 1818. Printed below is an excerpt of the relevant portion of his letter:

> In the year 1803, I was sergeant in the service of the Hudson's Bay Company, and in that capacity accompanied the late Louis in an incursion into the interior, with view to open a direct communication with the Indian nations immediately to the west of us. We left York fort

---

[24] The fort was also a trading post of the Hudson's Bay Company and was located in northeastern Manitoba at the mouth of the Hayes River. It had a staff of between 35-40 men.

ICE AGE

on the 19th of May 1803. About fortnight after, having been sent across a river, the name of which I do not now recollect, by Mr Louis's orders, the guide and myself suddenly came upon animal of an enormous size. It appeared about 20 feet in height, and had a very heavy and unwieldy appearance. I can give but a very lame account of it, on account the consternation into which I was thrown. The largeness of its belly was enormous, nearly touching the ground. Its colour was a dirty black. By Mr Louis's desire I attempted a drawing of it, which he got, but I am sure it could not have been very accurate. Mr Louis unfortunately saw only its footsteps and dung. He took correct measure of the former, which was about two feet square.[25]

As always, it's fascinating when witnesses from different time periods and locations give the same, unique details in their descriptions, even if they go against what is often accepted by science.

About four years after Fowler's account came yet another mammoth story, published in the *Alaskan* on March 4, 1893:

The Hunter's Story

The following is copied from an exchange received by the last mail from the Juneau Free Press, which paper passed out of existence some two years ago.

---

[25] http://www.strangehistory.net/2014/02/27/colonel-fowler-and-the-mammoth/

The Stikine Indians positively assert that within the last five years they have frequently seen animals which, from the description given, must be mastodons.

Last spring, while out hunting, one of their hunters came across a series of large tracks, each the size of the bottom of a salt barrel, sunk deep in the moss. He followed the curious trail for some miles, finally coming out in full view of his game. As a class these Indians are the bravest of hunters, but the proportions of this new species of game filled the hunter with terror, and he took to swift and immediate flight.

He describes the creature as being as large as a post trader's store, with great, shining, yellowish-white tusks and a mouth large enough to swallow a man at a single nip. He further states that the animal was undoubtedly of the same kind as those whose bones and tusks lie all over the country.

The fact that other hunters have told of seeing these monsters browsing on the herbs up along the river gives a certain probability to the story. Over on Fortymile Creek, bones of mastodons are quite plentiful. One ivory tusk nine feet long projects from one of the sand dunes on the creek, and single teeth have been found that are so large that they would have been a good load for a man to carry.

I believe that the mule-footed hog still exists, that live mastodons play tag with the aurora every night on Fortymile Creek in Alaska.

ICE AGE

Though I do believe there's a good case to be made that some mammoths survived into the 19th Century in certain regions, today, these remnant mammoths are most likely extinct. As to recent videos purporting to show mammoths in Siberia in 2012 and 2013, they were proven to be hoaxes.

Sources:

Beachcombing's Bizarre History Blog. "Colonel Fowler and the Mammoth, 1887." (February 27, 2014) http://www.strangehistory.net/2014/02/27/colonel-fowler-and-the-mammoth/

Benedict, Adam. *Monsters in Print: A Collection Of Curious Creatures Known Mostly From Newspapers.* Janesville: WI, 2019.

Schwarz, Rob. "Woolly Mammoth Sightings – Are These Prehistoric Creatures Still Alive?" Stranger Dimensions (January 18, 2018)
www.strangerdimensions.com/2018/01/18/woolly-mammoth-sightings/

Swancer, Brent. "Mysterious Encounters with Supposedly Extinct Ice Age Monsters." Mysterious Universe. (January 19, 2018)
mysteriousuniverse.org/2018/01/mysterious-encounters-with-supposedly-extinct-ice-age-monsters/

"SNAIK STORIES"
ROCKY MOUNTAIN MAMMOTHS?

☞ THE FOLLOWING letter was published in the *Scots Magazine* of June 1, 1818. It describes what sounds to be a mammoth...

REPORT OF THE EXISTENCE OF UNKNOWN ANIMAL OF VAST SIZE AMONG THE ROCKY MOUNTAINS OF NORTH AMERICA.

Mr. Editor, the following short notice relative to what seems to me to be a subject of no slight interest may probably be deemed worthy of insertion either among your customary memoranda of natural history, or in some vacant corner of your instructive miscellany. You know that specimens of what has been denominated the wool-bearing animal have lately been transmitted from the rocky mountains of North America, to the professor of natural history in this city. This animal had not been described in any of the great works on natural history; and though it is a remarkable quadruped, not only from its haunts, which are among the high precipices of stupendous mountains, but from the great beauty and value of its fleece, it has till within few years been altogether unknown to any of the numerous scientific individuals who have been so actively engaged in

ICE AGE

investigating the wonders of every quarter of the globe. The fact is, however, that this animal, which we are informed is intermediate between the goat and the antelope, has been long familiar the traders who traverse the immense wildernesses which encompass its haunts, and I have repeatedly heard descriptions of it from individuals of that profession, who were not aware that in this part of the world it was so great a curiosity. What I wish particularly to state at present, however, is, that, in the course of these conversations, I have received from the same individuals the most positive assurances of the existence of another animal among the same mountains, of immense size, and equally unknown certainly to the naturalists of Europe. The fact of its existence rests upon the testimony of two different parties who had been sent some errand into the interior valleys of those mountains. The first party came suddenly upon the animal in a deep and formerly unvisited recess, and were so alarmed at its prodigious size, (exceeding that of the largest elephant,) and at its unknown aspect, that they immediately retreated in great consternation to the encampment from which they had been dispatched. Another party was sent to the same spot to ascertain the fact; and though the animal was not observed, its footsteps could be distinctly traced, and each compartment of its hoof is stated to have admitted both the feet of the travellers. It ought to observed, that these parties were perfectly familiar with the appearance of the [sic] buffaloe which indeed they were in the daily habit of killing; and that the animal which they saw cannot therefore be regarded as an individual of that tribe. It was seen, too, as I have already stated, in a very remote and central valley, and the intervals between its paces are described having been of astonishing magnitude. Now we know well that animals of immense size have inhabited the northern parts of our earth in former times, and the huge remains which are every day dug up, are more likely to have belonged to individuals of such an animal as that now alluded to, than to any extinct species of a former world. Nor is there any part of the globe to which we should more naturally turn proofs of the continued existence of such animals, (if they do still exist,) than the immense mountains where this individual was seen. These mountains have been untrodden in many of their solitudes by any even of the savage nations that inhabit these regions, for I am informed, that these tribes have one path by which they uniformly descend from the great interior wildernesses, to the encampments of our traders, for the purpose of disposing of the produce of their chase; and the majestic grandeur and extreme solitude of the mountains themselves, seem to harmonize with the attributes of so wonderful an animal. I am well aware, at the same time, how strongly fear and amazement might operate in exciting the imagination of men who found themselves amidst the awful stillness of a region so remarkable in every respect, and how natural it was for them in these circumstances to give preternatural magnitude to some familiar but bulky animal. Yet when I reflect on the character and experience of the individuals by whom this relation was given, and on all the probabilities by which their assertion is supported, I confess, that I feel a strong inclination to give full credit to every particular of their testimony. You will also be aware, that the existence of such an animal, if well ascertained, would be one of the most interesting facts which it is possible in our present state of knowledge to acquire; and if the Ornithorinchus, or any small prowler of the lakes of New Holland, is beheld with wonder and preserved with care, with what overpowering amazement should we contemplate the image of a quadruped, surpassing, according to our present accounts, the largest and most formidable that either browse in silence beneath our primeval forests or roam unmolested in the deep valleys of the hottest and least frequented regions of the globe; and the existence of which would at the same go so far in illustrating some the darkest passages in the past history of this earth. My object, however, in transmitting to you this notice is simply to elicit such further information, either in the way of confirmation or denial as may set this interesting query on more certain grounds; and as many of the individuals employed either in the service of the Hudson's Bay or of the North West Company, are daily arriving in this country, I hope that this hint may draw from such of them are actually of the parties before a satisfactory account of their expedition and discovery.

I am yours truly, P.

Edinburgh, June 6, 1818.

COWBOYS & SAURIANS

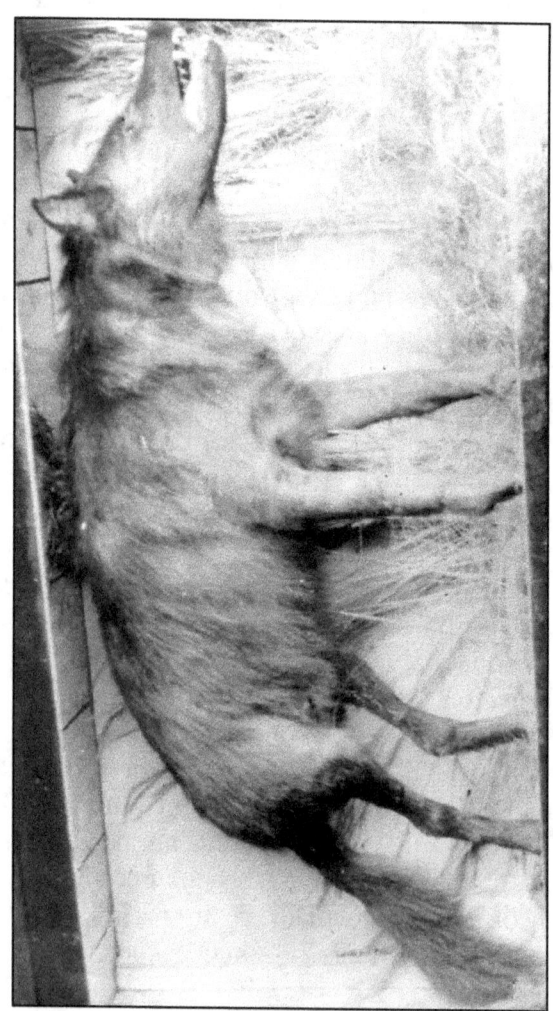

THE RINGDOCUS AKA THE SHUNKA WARAK'IN

8
SAGA OF THE SHUNKA WARAK'IN
MONTANA'S MYSTERY MONSTER

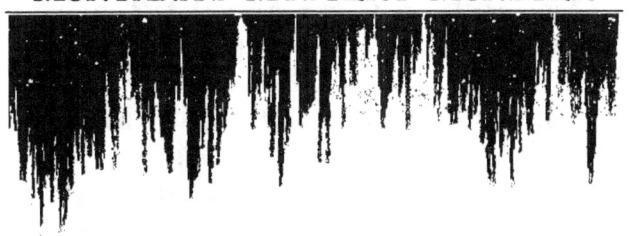

OF ALL THE STORIES in this book—and most of them are just that, stories—this one is the only one with proof to back it up. Because, in this case, there is actually a body...

Though our story predominantly takes place in Montana, we will start it out in Iowa, where the Ioway Native American tribe told tales of something called the *shunka warak'in*—the name literally meaning "carries off dogs." The hyena-like beast would sneak into their camps at night and—as the name implies—kill and carry away dogs.

Researcher Lance M. Foster managed to find some of the older accounts of the shunka warak'in thanks to notes taken on the subject by Alanson Skinner. In the early 1900s, Skinner heard the tales of the strange animal first hand from the Ioway Indians. The tales came from Chief David Tohee and Joseph Springer and told of the tribesmen killing a strange animal and keeping its skin. Skinner wrote the following in his "Ethnology of the Ioway Indians" published in 1926:

> One time the people began to miss their dogs. Every morning a few were gone, and no one knew the cause. Some thought it the work of an enemy, so the young men got up a war party and hid themselves so as to surprise and kill the nightly visitor. It turned out to be a strange animal, different from anything they had ever seen before. They named it "Carrying-off-dogs," but it is very like the animal the white people keep in their shows today and call hyena. When it entered the camp, the young warriors attacked it just as if it was a person. Again and again they shot at this creature, and could not kill it, but after following it a day and a half they at last succeeded in putting it to death. When it died, it cried just like a human being. When they heard this, and thought of the hard time they had in killing it, they decided that it must be a creature of great power. So they skinned it, and painted its hide, and later placed the hide in with the other powerful objects in the war bundle, to wear in battle across the shoulder to turn away flying bullets and arrows. But before the hide was put in the bundle, a big dance was held. Immediately afterward a party set out and were very successful, as they killed a number of

enemies, returning with many scalps. (Skinner 1926: 211-212).[26]

Unfortunately, the hide of this animal cannot be found today. However, in Montana, one of the creatures was killed in 1886 by Israel Hutchins. The Hutchins family arrived in the Madison River Valley in Montana by covered wagon in the 1880s. Hutchins had been searching for gold all across the U.S. until finally his wife put a stop to it and insisted that the family finally settle down. There the Mormon settlers established a model ranch, located about 40 miles from the town of Ennis. Eventually, they would be the recipient of a very strange visitor.

The man's grandson, Ross Hutchins, wrote about the incident many years later in his book *Trails to Nature's Mysteries: The Life of a Working Naturalist.*

Strange things often happened in the wild area where our ranch was located. One winter morning my grandfather was aroused by the barking of dogs. He discovered that a wolf-like beast of dark color was chasing my grandmother's geese. He fired his gun at the animal but missed. It ran off down the river, but several mornings later it was seen again at about dawn. It was seen several more times at the

---

[26] Foster, "Shunka Warak'in: A Mystery in Plain Sight," http://paranormalmontana.blogspot.com/2009/03/shunka-warakin.html

home ranch as well as at other ranches ten or fifteen miles down the valley. Whatever it was, it was a great traveler...

Those who got a good look at the beast described it as being nearly black and having high shoulders and a back that sloped downward like a hyena. Then one morning in late January, my grandfather was alerted by the dogs, and this time he was able to kill it. Just what the animal was is still an open question. After being killed, it was donated to a man named [Joseph] Sherwood who kept a combination grocery and museum at Henry Lake in Idaho.[27] It was mounted and displayed there for many years. He called it "ringdocus."[28]

And there the ringdocus sat for nearly 100 years. Then, in the 1980s, it mysteriously disappeared. In 1987, a book entitled *Just West of Yellowstone: A Guide to Exploring and Camping* was written by a landscape architect named Rae Ellen Moore. She wrote of seeing the mount of a strange hyena-like animal in a small museum in Henry's Lake, Idaho. Lucky for us, shunka warak'in researcher Lance M. Foster read the book and connected the dots.

Foster did some digging and was disappointed to learn that the museum had closed down, and no one knew what had happened to the taxidermy

---

[27] Other sources say Hutchins traded it to Sherwood for a cow.
[28] Hutchins, *Trails to Nature's Mysteries*, pp.50.

ICE AGE

collection there either. Around this time, Foster also drew parallels between the shunka warak'in of Iowa and the Ringdocus of Montana. He wrote to famed cryptozoologist Loren Coleman about the strange creatures. Coleman, in turn, wrote about it in his book *Cryptozoology A to Z* in 1999, reigniting interest in the old cryptid and its missing mount.

BOROPHAGUS BY CHARLES KNIGHT C.1902.

Coleman and Foster both speculated that it could be a type of prehistoric hyena. Coleman theorized that it could be a Borophagus, a type of hyena-like dog from the Pleistocene epoch. The Borophagus had powerful, bone-crushing jaws and was essentially built like a coyote on steroids. Scientists speculated that it was probably a scavenger just like modern hyenas.

COWBOYS & SAURIANS

Together Foster and Coleman did their best to find the old taxidermy mount, even getting confirmation that the Idaho Museum of Natural History did indeed acquire the Sherwood mounts from Henry's Lake, Idaho.

However, Coleman and Foster were beaten to the rediscovery of the mount by a likely source: a grandson of Israel Hutchins named Jack Kirby! Kirby had managed to find the mount in the Idaho Museum of Natural History and had even got them to loan it to him.

One of the first things Kirby did was take the mount to the grave of his grandfather, to tell him that they had brought the mystery creature home. The discovery at long last also managed to confirm the exact dimensions of the animal. An article on the discovery reported that, "It measures 48 inches from the tip of its snout to its rump, not including the tail, and stands from 27 to 28 inches high at the shoulder."[29]

In May of 2007, the specimen was put on display in the recently reopened Madison Valley History Museum. When asked to submit the creature for DNA testing to determine what it was, Kirby declined, wanting to let the mystery linger. His remark: "Do we want to know?"

Soon after the animal's return to Montana, the Island Park Historical Society of Idaho expressed concern that they may never get the old mount

---

[29] www.bozemandailychronicle.com/news/mystery-monster-returns-home-after-years/article_461c6958-ea1e-5f57-bee9-a3c11b0a18a6.html

back. The group wished to have it displayed at the John Sack cabin in Island Park.

Further confusing the matter is an alternate story that claims the beast was really shot and killed in Idaho, at a spot called Mack's Inn on the banks of the Snake River. Harold Bishop, a Mack's Inn resident, was researching the animal for a scout project. Over the course of his research, he interviewed a man named Pete Marx, who insisted the animal was shot by a range rider named Heini Schooster with a lever-action .32 special.

As is typical of cryptids, the ringdocus just continues to confuse rather than enlighten...

Sources:

Foster, Lance. "Shunka Warak'in: A Mystery in Plain Sight." Paranormal Montana. (March 3, 2009) http://paranormalmontana.blogspot.com/2009/03/shunka-warakin.html

Hutchins, Ross. *Trails to Nature's Mysteries.* New York, NY: Dodd, Mead & Company, 1977.

Williams, Walt. "Mystery monster returns home after 121 years." *Bozeman Daily Chronicle.* (November 14, 2007)
https://www.bozemandailychronicle.com/news/mystery-monster-returns-home-after-

years/article_461c6958-ea1e-5f57-bee9-a3c11b0a18a6.html

FIRST PUBLISHED RESTORATION OF
ELASMOTHERIUM BY RASHEVSKY C.
1878.

9
PREHISTORIC RHINOCEROS
A "STRANGE ANIMAL" IN COLORADO

IN THE WORLD OF cryptozoology, there aren't too many cryptids in the Rhinocerotidae family. In fact, there's only one significant example, and it turned out to be a real animal. Enter the Northern White Rhinoceros (aka the Northern Square-Lipped Rhinoceros), which was thought to be a myth until it was discovered in Central Africa in 1900. Today, there are sadly only two members of this species still living.

All the way over in Pueblo, Colorado, a rhino-cryptid, possibly of the prehistoric variety, was sighted in the early 1870s. The story appeared on page one of the *Marysville Tribune* on January 18, 1871.

COWBOYS & SAURIANS

A Strange Animal
[From the Pueblo (Colorado) Chieftain]

That there exists in the mountains of Colorado beasts and animals unknown to the devotees of science, there cannot be the least shadow of a doubt. We just learned of a trapper on the Greenhorn, a stream about twenty miles south of Pueblo, who while hunting recently for elk and deer, saw a strange animal at the sight of which he was not only astonished, but at first it caused him great fear. The hunter was, however, in a position that afforded him protection, and after the first surprise, and had gained an assurance of safety, he watched the beast, and the following is the description he gives of the thing: It was larger than an ox, and of a kind of mouse color, with a skin varied with light stripes similar to those of a zebra. Its head favored that of a rhinoceros, but much larger, and a bushy tail like that of a fox. The animal fed on grass, weeds, etc., and finally disappeared, crossing the creek and going up the mountains, where it is likely the brute has habitation of some kind. The next day our informant examined the tracks of this singular looking animal, and found them to be like those of a horse, but a great deal larger. We cannot but believe the assertions of the trapper to be entirely true, as the whole story is corroborated by Mr. Matt Riddlebarger, who lives in that neighborhood, and who has seen the same beast or one like it. He thinks that by the next issue of

ICE AGE

our paper we will be able to give more authentic information on this matter, as we learn that a posse of gentlemen are now in pursuit of this seeming monstrosity, and who are determined to capture or kill the animal, and thus give to the world and science another proof that there are still strange animals in existence, which although scarce, are not entirely extinct.

ILLUSTRATION OF ELASMOTHERIUM BY CHARLES KNIGHT.

The closest example of megafauna that this "strange animal" from the article resembles would have to be either an Elasmotherium or a Coelodonta. It's hard to say for sure because the account is a bit lacking in description. For instance, it says that its head "favored that of a rhinoceros," but it doesn't confirm whether or not it had a horn.

But, considering a rhino's nasal horn is its most distinct attribute, it's safe to assume that's what the witness meant. The other slightly frustrating aspect of the sighting is the size of the creature being described as "larger than an ox." How much larger exactly? Presumably, they meant that it was close in size to an ox but slightly larger.

The description given seems closer to an Elasmotherium, which notably had a much bigger horn than a Coelodonta, whose horn was closer in size to a regular rhino's. The Elasmotherium was much larger than an ox, though, at six feet high by 16 feet long in some cases. But what the man saw could have been a smaller specimen. The Coelodonta, on the other hand, was nearer the size of an ox. In either case, both animals were grass eaters (remember, the animal in the article was observed eating grass). Both animals also had a covering of fur on their bodies.

Where the account becomes problematic when trying to match this to a prehistoric rhinoceros are the feet. Tracks left behind by the animal were compared to that of a horse's hooves, which is not comparable to a three-toed rhino. One way in which the trapper could have compared them to the tracks of a horse is that the animal's feet were somewhat round. There is another prehistoric, rhino-like mammal that could match the description and that has very rounded feet (similar to an elephant but smaller) with less prominent toes compared to the Elasmotherium. This animal would be the Arsinotherium, which had two prominent nasal horns (though it is not part of the

ICE AGE

Rhinocerotidae family).[30] However, if it was such a creature, surely witnesses would have compared it to a two-horned rhino.

Also uncharacteristic of a rhino was the bushy tail that the trapper compared to a fox. Rhinos have tails, certainly, and the Elasmotherium and Coelodonta both had slightly hairier tails than a modern-day rhino, but they wouldn't be considered bushy in comparison to a fox. Therefore it's possible this creature was a heretofore undiscovered animal entirely.[31]

Having examined the cryptid itself, let us now try to identify the one witness that was named: Matt Riddlebarger. Results for Riddlebarger are encouraging overall. According to the *House Journal of the Legislative Assembly of the Territory of Colorado* published in 1861, Matt Riddlebarger was nominated to be the Public Printer (though he did not win). Eventually, Riddlebarger became a judge, as evidenced by another edition of the *House Journal* published in 1867. There he is referred to as the Honorable Matt Riddlebarger and was elected to fill a seat in the Territorial House. Other sources list Riddlebarger as an attorney at one point and also a postmaster.

---

[30] The horns of a Arsinotherium were hollow and also contained blood vessels.

[31] As far as it being an animal made up by the article's writer, it's not a very fantastic story. The made up stories are usually a bit more adventurous, and the creatures more fantastic in nature. This would seem to be a real cryptid sighting in my opinion.

In 1862, he had been an owner of the *Mountaineer*, a "wandering press" as it was called. This could almost be taken as a negative to our story, though, as this shows that Riddlebarger had a history of sorts in newspapers (and knew the importance of selling them).

As our key witness was both a judge and a newspaper editor, it makes this story rather hard to validate. Nor are there many sightings of rhino-like cryptids across the world, let alone near Pueblo, Colorado.[32]

Sources:
Colorado (Territory) Legislative Assembly House. *House Journal of the Legislative Assembly of the Territory of Colorado.* (1861).

Gladden, Sanford. *Early Days of Boulder, Colorado Vol I.* (1982).

---

[32] One of the lone exceptions is the Karkadann, a cryptid native to Persia and Northern Africa. It too is believed to be an Elasmotherium.

"SNAIK STORIES"
THE MAMMOTH'S GHOST?

☞ MAYBE I'M grasping at straws, but any Fortean researcher has to be interested in this ghost sighting from Alma, Colorado, from 1908. In the sighting, witnesses described a giant elephant ghost that shot flames from its trunk! As the regular elephant was not native to North America, it could have only been the ghost of a mammoth... if it was anything at all other than a figment of someone's imagination, that is.

The following article was reprinted (sans the exact date and paper of origin) on MyteriousUniverse.org in regards to Spring Heeled Jack sightings (it was included because the ghost here breathed fire similar to Spring-Heeled Jack):

> Alma had a sensation this week in the shape of a ghost, which appeared at night. People coming from the saloons about midnight saw a strange sight, or imagined they did. One night the phantom was seen near the Thomas saloon, another time it was at the bridge on Main Street. The courageous Almaites gave chase, but when they arrived at the spot the apparition had mysteriously disappeared. Some describe it as a beautiful woman, clad in the finest white lingerie. The spot where the beauty disappeared

was fragrant with the perfume of roses and violets.

Others again say it looked to them like a huge elephant, with streams of fire issuing from its trunk, and when they arrived at the spot where it had vanished, the smell of sulfur and brimstone permeated the air. The young ladies of Alma are frightened and will not venture forth in the evening without an escort. The gallant young men act with the greatest of pleasure in this capacity. So far, the 'spook' has not been caught, but it this should be the case, would summarily be dealt with.

[https://mysteriousuniverse.org/2013/10/spring-heeled-jack-in-america/]

10
THE GIANT SEA COBRA
ATTACK OF THE ALASKAN SEA SERPENT

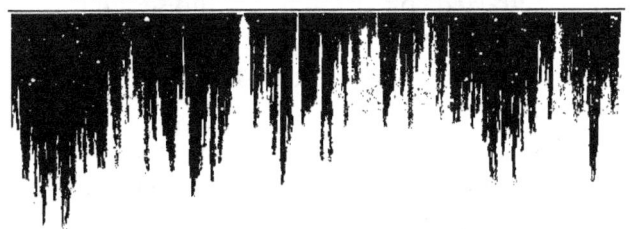

THE FOLLOWING STORY is far too fantastic to be true. In fact, it's one of the most exciting cryptid encounters that I have ever read. Being set in Alaska, still a place of mystery for most Americans in the late 1800s, it was the perfect place to set a tall tale. And yet, I was also shocked to confirm that one of the men involved, S.A. Keller, was a real person, but we'll get to that later. First, here is the story as it appeared in the *Juneau City Mining Record* on June 25, 1894:

> Here is the story as related by these two daring hunters. "When we had reached a spot nearly across the mouth of Lossen Creek which flows into Gastineau Channel," began Jack Ross, "Mr.

Keller expressed a desire to go ashore and look up some old landmarks that he had established on a former pedestrian cruise around the island.

Keller was about to go ashore when he espied two large eagles perched upon a hemlock tree nearby. He instantly seized his rifle and shotgun and started in pursuit of them, but he had no sooner set his foot on shore when his attention was attracted by an unusual noise and on looking around a sight met his eyes that paralyzed him and caused him to drop his weapons."

"On my port quarter," continued Keller, "about three quarters of a mile distant, there loomed the swaying neck and head of some monster unlike anything I had ever seen or dreamed of in all my life, and I have had some terrible experiences. With its head more than ten feet in the air, the monster was swimming directly toward us with fearful velocity, while the mighty throes of his extended body emitted a sound not unlike that caused by the pounding of a side-wheel steamer's paddle.

"My first impulse after regaining my self-control," continued Mr. Keller, "was to reach for my shotgun, but in my excitement, I had strayed some twenty yards from where I had dropped my arms... I had miscalculated the speed of the great serpent. While some distance from my gun, I heard a howl of agony from Jack, and looking over my shoulder, I instinctively fetched a shriek of horror and despair.

ICE AGE

While I was going less than twenty feet, the monster had glided up and pounced upon Jack. Now Jack, as you know, weighs fully 150 pounds and this green-eyed captor was holding him in his mouth more than twenty feet in the air.

I don't know how I reached the gun, but in less time than it takes to record it, I had seized the gun and sent a heavy charge of buckshot into the creature's belly about where it emerged from the water.

A visible tremor passed through his body; his head fell down, bringing Jack down with frightful velocity. The poor fellow was hurled against the side of the boat with a force, as I thought, that would kill him instantly, and landing the ax he had in his hand far out on dry land.

It was now apparent that my shot had not only wounded the monster but had angered him to a rather dangerous and alarming degree. Instantly his head was again on high, deafening hisses came from his throat, and the waters for a hundred feet seaward were churned into foam by the horrid writhing of his body.

Again I raised my gun and discharged the other barrel. If my first shot had angered him, my second shot worked him into a frenzy that knew no bounds.

Throwing back his great hooded head in true serpentine style, he began to strike at our boat. At one time fastening his jaws upon our starboard gunwale, he quickly wrenched off a piece of solid timber five feet long and two inches thick, as easily, apparently, as a man would a piece of paper. Throwing his body into a series of great vertical coils eight feet in diameter, he completely encircled the boat, and with one constriction crushed it into a shapeless mass.

After crushing the boat the monster did not immediately uncoil himself, but lay some minutes with fragments still in his embrace, while his ever-restless tail whipped the surface of the sea. In one of its gyrations the end of the tail fell upon the beach and, with what must have been superhuman agility, I seized the ax that had been hurled from Jack's clutch, and with one blow cut off ten or fifteen feet of the wriggling end. I was esteeming this a most valuable prize, but before I could secure it the slimy mass wriggled into the water and was lost.

From this time the great monster evidently began to weaken from loss of blood, which was pouring in streams from his head and the wound given him by the ax. Slowly regaining his normal position in the water, the creature withdrew toward the open sea and was soon out of sight.

When I first saw him swimming squarely abreast of me, I should judge from the elevated head to where the sea was lashed by the end of his tail the distance was 200 feet. The great flattened head was hooded like that of an East Indian cobra, and from the tip of the nose to the insertion of the neck would have measured five feet. The head was fully three feet wide, but

ICE AGE

appeared to be deficient in vertical depth. The eyes were set just forward of the hooded appendage and were as large as the eyes of an ox. There were no indications of a dorsal fin or rudimental feet, as have been attributed by some former observers to the so-called sea monsters. But Jack claimed he had very large horns.

After several hours of work and administering several doses of medicine, Jack was brought around all right. From the nature of the wounds inflicted upon Jack it was apparent the monster was not venomous.

If this story actually happened, I highly doubt that Jack Ross could have survived a bite from such a creature, even if it was non-venomous. And though I tried to find records of existence for Ross (in particular, a death record not long after this story), I found nothing.

However, as to Mr. Ross, I should point out that I first came across this story in an excellent book by Ed Ferrell called *Strange Stories of Alaska and the Yukon*. Mr. Ferrell begins his chapters with a bit of background information and lists some details about Ross not present in the article. Specifically, Ferrell says that Ross was a Deputy Marshall in Douglas City, Alaska.

What really got me, though, was when I searched for records on S.A. Keller. In the book *Report of the Commissioner of Education, Volume 2* (published in 1896), I found mention of S.A.

COWBOYS & SAURIANS

Keller as a teacher in Douglas City between 1893 and 1894, when this story was written.

With that information now in hand, I have to wonder, did a school teacher and a deputy tangle with a giant sea cobra? Or, perhaps, did Keller write this exciting story to entertain his students? I would imagine the latter option is more likely, but you never know...

Sources:

Ferrell, *Strange Stories of Alaska and the Yukon.* Fairbanks, AK: Epicenter Press, 1996.

United States Office of Education. *Report of the Commissioner of Education, Volume 2.* 1896.

11
MACFARLANE'S BEAR
AND OTHER BEAR CRYPTIDS

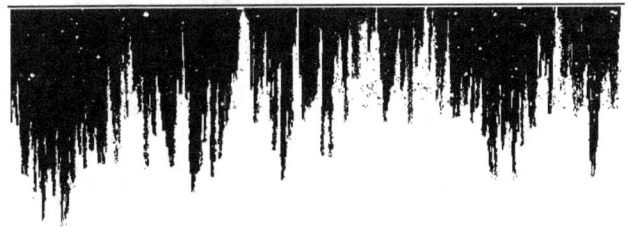

AFTER THE GREAT SUCCESS of *Jaws* in 1975, many other studios decided to unleash their own giant "animals attack" movies. One of the most notorious *Jaws* copycats was *Grizzly*, which featured a 17-foot tall bear attacking campers in the woods. To explain the bear's immense size, one of the characters claimed that it was a prehistoric survivor, left over from the Ice Age.

The biggest and baddest of the prehistoric bears was the South American giant short-faced bear (*Arctotherium angustidens*), which stood 12 feet tall. In North America, the best-known bear-cryptid, and a possible prehistoric survivor, is "MacFarlane's Bear." In 1864, Inuit hunters in Canada's Northwestern Territory shot and killed an exceptionally large specimen of bear. It was also unusual in that it had yellow fur. Furthermore, the skull was oddly misshapen and had unusual teeth that weren't typical of a normal bear. The Inuits further claimed that the bear was massive and was very rarely seen (and only then in remote areas).

PRIMITIVE MAN ATTACKING THE CAVE BEAR C.1870s.

The skin of the carcass was given to the naturalist Robert MacFarlane, who, in turn, shipped the strange specimen off to the Smithsonian. The sample was then placed in storage and was forgotten until it was rediscovered by Dr. Clinton Hart Merriam in 1918. Dr. Merriam felt that the bear had been shot too far out of the normal range for a brown bear. Dr. Merriam proposed that it could be a brand new species and named it *Vetularctos inopinatus*, ("ancient unexpected bear").

ICE AGE

Though some speculate that this was a prehistoric survivor of some sort, others have suggested it was merely a grizzly-polar bear hybrid, which is possible. There are plans to do a DNA test to compare the skull to that of a grizzly-polar bear hybrid—if the Smithsonian allows it, and so far they have not. This should come as no surprise though, as there are conspiracy theories that the Smithsonian Institute does everything in their power to cover up the existence of prehistoric survivors.

However, in an episode of the History Channel's *Monster Quest* series, paleontologist Dr. Blaine W. Schubert was allowed by the Smithsonian to examine the skull (though they did not allow it to be filmed). Discouragingly, Schubert claimed he was certain that "it was the skull of a young, female brown bear" and "actually, not a particularly large individual."

But, we must ask, were there any other sightings of MacFarlane's bear before or after 1864? The noted writer and sportsman Caspar Whitney claimed that he saw an odd-looking bear in the late 1800s. He wrote the following of the sighting:

It is a peculiar looking bear, seeming a cross between the grizzly and the polar, and it has this peculiarity, that its hind claws are as big as the fore claws, while its head looks somewhat like that of an Eskimo dog, very broad in the forehead, with square, long muzzle, and ears set on quite like the dog's. It is very wide at the shoulders, and its robe in color resembles the grizzly.[33]

CASPAR WHITNEY.

John "Grizzly" Adams, the famous "mountain man" and bear trainer, came across several cryptid bears during his travels. Once, he captured an especially large grizzly weighing 1,510 pounds!

---

[33] Swancer, "Mysterious Encounters with Supposedly Extinct Ice Age Monsters," MysteriousUniverse.org.

ICE AGE

More notable though, was his observation in the wild of a bear with quills like a hedgehog! It's also possible that Adams, in this case, just wanted to tell a tall tale.

ADAMS AND BEN FRANKLIN

Sources:

Swancer, "Mysterious Encounters with Supposedly Extinct Ice Age Monsters," *Mysterious Universe.org.* https://mysteriousuniverse.org/2018/01/mysterious-encounters-with-supposedly-extinct-ice-age-monsters/

12
A MYSTERY MONSTER
MONSTER OR PREHISTORIC MOOSE?

THE FOLLOWING is another of those strange tales where it is difficult to discern just what the witness is talking about—mostly because what they are describing doesn't seem to line up with anything in the history books, prehistoric or otherwise. The story was published in the *Jonesboro Flag and Advertiser* on March 1, 1873:

A NONDESCRIPT.
A Strange Animal Running Wild in Tennessee—Superstitious Fright of the People—An Escape
The Devil After Brownlow.

A gentleman recently from the Shelton Laurel District informs us that the people in that "densely thicketed" country are greatly excited in regard to the appearance, upon several different occasions and in several different places, of a huge mountain monster, the species of which is unknown. Mr. George Anderson, one of the gentlemen residing in the Laurel country, being one of the persons who saw the monster, also furnishes us with the following description of it:

"I was out in the jungle hunting up some lost hogs, when all of a sudden there came into my path a beast, the appearance of which, I must confess, caused me to quake for the first time in my many years. Aside from its strange and unusual appearance, the unearthly yell it uttered on perceiving me, which reverberated and reverberated through the forest, was enough to shake the senses of the most daring adventurer. The animal was some hundred yards distant from me, and appeared to be a huge black bear with mane and head like a lion, but had horns like an elk upon it. Its tail was long and bushy, with dark and light rings around it to its very extremity. Its eyes gleamed like a panther's, and its size was that of an ordinary ox, but somewhat longer. Just previous to making its appearance I had shot off my gun at a squirrel, and felt little prepared to meet such a ferocious beast without any weapon of defense. I immediately set about reloading my rifle, but had scarcely begun when it started toward me. I retreated in as good an order as possible, and must say I did some good running—not looking back until I had reached

ICE AGE

an open spot, when I found the animal had disappeared in the laurel thicket. This is no story, Mr. Editor, gotten up to scare naughty children. I am not the only one who has seen the monster. Several have seen it since I did; and, as sheep and calves are lately missing, it is presumed to be a carnivorous brute. Many have fortified their homes to prevent a night attack from the strange monster, the like of which was never seen in these mountains before. Some think it has escaped from some rambling menagerie, while others superstitiously think it is sent to warn the people of some great approaching danger.
—Jonesboro (Tenn.) Flag and Advertiser, 14th.

Frankly, nothing exists like what Mr. Anderson saw. However, it's important to note that he observed it from a distance. So, perhaps we can forgive his description that makes it an amalgam of unrelated animals. The most notable detail was the "horns like an elk," or antlers. Therefore the creature is limited to only a few species of animals that possess antlers. The closest megafauna that this description matches is the Sivatherium, an animal from a suborder of giraffids. In some restorations, it is portrayed as having an extra cropping of mangy hair around its neck and shoulders, which could explain the "mane" that Anderson saw. The size of the animal would be about right as well.

As to blaming the disappearance of other animals on this creature, that was possibly just circumstantial. It would be different if Anderson had seen the creature killing and eating another animal. As far as the witness was concerned, the creature looked monstrous and, therefore, must have behaved like a monster.

SIVATHERIUM RESTORATION C.1896.

It should be noted, however, that the Sivatherium never roamed North America. The reconstruction above is also now considered outdated, and the neck of the creature was slightly longer than what is depicted here.

There are no notable cryptid sightings of anything resembling a Sivatherium today. However, Karl Shuker discusses artifacts that seem to imply that the Sivatherium survived long past its expiration date in *Still in Search of Prehistoric Survivors.*

13

ICE FISHING WITH A SEA SERPENT

A SNOWY SEA SNAKE

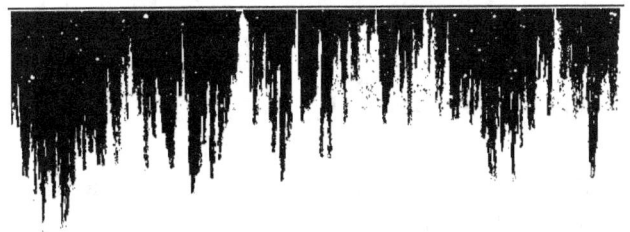

SEA SERPENT stories are a dime a dozen. And, once you've read a dozen of them, they can get a little monotonous. Usually, they amount to someone seeing a strange, serpentine creature in the water: end of story. And then, every so often, you run across a wild tale like this. It was published in the *Decatur Wise County Messenger* on July 23, 1892.

THE HIDEOUS MONSTER.
That Startled a Fisherman at Chain Lake, Maine

That the Chain Lake serpent which had been the subject of many stirring yarns from Washington county had subsided was believed generally, but the monster has started on the warpath again, and a party of fifteen bold hunters started out from Whitneyville recently to lay him low, writes a Bangor correspondent of the New York Sun. About ninety feet in length by three feet in breadth of beam are the general dimensions that were given by a man who saw it cross the lake at railroad speed three years ago, and that estimate was declared to be very nearly correct by other parties who saw the monster's trail in the mud on the shore.

The latest news of the snake is furnished by Clarence S. Lunt who went to Chain Lake on a fishing trip. Arriving at the lake early in the day he chiseled a hole about a foot square in the ice, set his line; and was filling his pipe when there was a shock such as would be caused by a log falling upon the ice. A second shock came soon, and the water in the fish hole began to boil. Suddenly, to the horror of the fisherman, a most hideous head was thrust up through the hole. It was a long black, flat-shaped scaly snout, changing to a smooth, oily gray under the lower jaws. The mouth had rows of saw-like teeth and it opened and shut convulsively. At intervals a great red tongue of the brilliancy of flame ran out and as the head rolled from side to side in vain efforts to force its way further through the aperture in the ice it emitted great flecks of spume of a dense, sickening odor. The head protruded about fifteen inches above the ice, but no eyes were visible, and Lunt is certain that they were below the surface, for the creature

ICE AGE

must have eyes, else it could not have found the fish hole. The monster struggled fearfully for a few minutes and then withdrew. Lunt sat down on the ice completely unnerved by his experience, and it was some time before he could muster sufficient strength to walk home. He had proceeded only a short distance when he heard the same commotion as at first, and, looking back, he saw the hideous head protruding again from the hole. Then he fled, and he cannot be induced to go back to Chain lake.

Great excitement was caused by Lunt's story of the monster, and some persons were unkind enough to drop remarks about the increasing consumption of Portland whisky in those parts, saying that the article smuggled in from New Brunswick was better. But many believe in the existence of the reptile.

First off, Lunt was a real man, born in Maine in 1867. There's only one problem with Lunt: he was a newspaper editor. And if there's one thing a Golden Age newspaper editor knew, it was the value of selling papers.

See this excerpt from *The Beta Theta Pi, Volume 17*:

—One of the most pleasing of Bangor's (Me.) society events this season was the wedding of Miss Edith Mary Prescott and Mr. Clarence S. Lunt, Maine State, '84, at St. John's Episcopal Church, October 22nd, 1889. Mr. Lunt has been city editor of the Bangor Daily Commercial for the past two years, and has won for himself a most enviable reputation among the rising young journalists of Maine.

Furthermore—and you can consider this either encouraging or discouraging towards the story's validity—the Chain Lake monster was an established cryptid by 1892 (in other words, an established cryptid that Lund could use in his tall tale). The sightings date back to the Native American legends of the Algonquin Indians, but the creature was first reported by settlers in a newspaper in 1880. The book, *America's Loch Ness Monsters*, reprints the relevant portion of the article:

The description given by the correspondent of this monster snake is startling. It was as large, he says, as a very large piling, and about fifty feet long and carried its head as high as a man when standing up... It did not change its course for any obstacle either on land or water. It was heard from in several places, still going on in the same direction. It doubtless came from Chain Lakes, as that seems to be the place which is inhabited by such monsters.[34]

Despite that account, reports in later years cast doubt upon the monster's existence, notably in the March 21, 1882 edition of the *Machias Union* in

---

[34] Rife, *America's Loch Ness Monsters*, pp.9.

ICE AGE

the form of a letter by Sewell S. Quimby of Wesley. The Alexander-Crawford Historical Society researched the matter and established that Quimby was a real man who operated a sawmill along the Chain Lake Stream in the early 1880s. His letter goes as follows:

"Mr. Editor: As I was returning home Saturday night I heard a man say with great earnestness that he had seen the man that saw the great snake, and that they were going to lease the ground around Chain Lakes for a hunting ground; that they were already having great chains made, huge traps constructed, harpoons, lances, spears, gaffs and barbs in readiness when the spring opened, and were going to capture if possible the monster of the mighty deep, now landlocked in the small fresh water ponds of the Machias Chain Lakes.

Just a little later I heard another person say, with the same vim, they had seen a man that saw the man that said he saw the great snake. ... Hall and Libby were on the shore of Chain Lake ... they heard a noise ... and saw what they took to be a man and a skiff, but soon became convinced it was a serpent ... its smallest part was as large as a pork barrel. He says when last seen in the outlet, it had left the water and passed a distant point of land covered with granite boulders."[35]

---

[35] www.mainething.com/alexander/memories/POCOMOONSHINE%20LAKE%20MONSTER.htm

COWBOYS & SAURIANS

Quimby then goes on to refute the claims of Hall and Libby, stating that he was at Chain Lake that very same day and saw no monster. His main point of contention was that there were no granite boulders on the lakeshore, therefore if the men described the geography of the shore incorrectly, then they likely saw no monster either.

Quimby did investigate another serious claim of the monster though, that might have shown physical evidence:

> In January, one Hunnewell of Alexander came to our camp with a big story that he had seen the trail of the huge creature, four feet wide, three feet deep and a quarter mile long. Logs had been turned out of his track and he had torn things up awfully. Mr. H. was also very much excited.[36]

Quimby again took a skeptical angle on the alleged evidence. He believed that the tracks were simply the result of the swamp thawing out. The Alexander-Crawford Historical Society writes:

> Quimby estimated it to be between 3 and 4 feet wide and 2 ½ to 3 feet deep. The trail was sinuous, making 3 or 4 bends. It was in two places, each 3 rods long, and looked a little particular. All this Quimby attributed to the freezing and thawing of the swamp...[37]

---

[36] Ibid.
[37] Ibid.

ICE AGE

So far, things are not looking good for the Chain Lake monster's validity. Further damning was a 1907 article printed in the *Washington Post* on May 12th. It begins with various, humorous legends about how the beast began—many of them involving liquor. And yet, the scathing article does take the time to present an in-depth, serious description as given by the witnesses over the years:

It has no scales or armor belt on its body, no sharp saw teeth on its back, and no horns on its head. At no time has it ever been seen to breathe fire, or to conceal itself from view by clouds of smoke manufactured for that purpose. At no public occasion has it roared like an angry bull or screamed like a siren whistle on a steam yacht. It has unfolded no leathery wings, and except in a very few cases it has deported itself, in every particular, like a huge and self-respecting snake.

Reports as to the size of the serpent differ widely, some making it out to be no more than 80 or 100 feet in length and girthing no more than a flour barrel, while other eyewitnesses have said it was fully 500 feet long and as big around as a high-pressure standpipe.

Its color is an olive green which gives out suggestions of rainbow tints when the sun shines brightly. Concerning the dental formula of the creature, or whether it has any teeth at all, there is no evidence available.

IMAGE ACCOMPANYING THE
WASHINGTON POST ARTICLE

ICE AGE

On solid ice or on land, it travels by forming its flexible body into vertical arches instead of lateral hoops. At intervals of about 25 feet in its length, two large, flat flippers or feet are attached to the underside... Those who claim to have seen the tracks declare they are ten feet in diameter and resemble the enlarged imprints made by the feet of geese and ducks. This leads to the presumption that the attachments may be used as flippers to assist in swimming when in the lakes.

The article then dovetails into what appears to be a real horror story...

The most serious charge preferred against the great serpent was the abduction and detention of John Wesley Ackley. The victim was a young man who lived with his uncle and aunt on a farm near the swampy shores of Chain Lakes. The youth had been without profitable employment for several months until his uncle offered to pay him $1 a hundred for all the sizeable and straight brown ash hoop poles he would cut and put into bundles. As poles of this kind sold for $2.50 a hundred in the Calais market and the stumpage cost nothing the uncle and nephew were making a good living, the boy doing the cutting and bundling and the old man marketing the product.

One morning in February the youth took breakfast by lamplight, and, carrying his ax and dinner pail, started for the shores of the lakes to resume his labors. The boy did not return at night for supper. Next morning, when his Uncle Charles went to the chopping for another load of poles, he took two neighbors along to assist in the search.

On a dry knoll, close to the water of the lake they found the empty dinner pail of the missing youth. Sticking in the stump of a tree back of the spot where a fire had been kindled, was the boy's ax. On the soft ice of the lake, leading from an open hole of the knoll were great splaying tracks of the Chain Lakes serpent.

Nobody doubted that the snake had swallowed the youth. The boy had been at the edge of the lake at the time, and the snake had resided in the lake for many years, thus demonstrating that the snake had what the lawyers term an "exclusive opportunity." Another and more convincing argument in favor of the tragedy theory was that his uncle was owing the boy $8.43 at the time he disappeared, and it was contrary to nature for anybody to run away leaving so much money uncollected.

For some reason—possibly because there was no remains to honor—no funeral services were held, though some talk has been made about erecting a monument to the memory of the youth.

Whatever mystery there was concerning the young man was explained. In 1899, when he returned to his uncle's home for a short visit. He had learned a trade and was at that time working in a machine shop at Manchester, N. H. He had never seen any serpent and was shocked to learn that he was dead.

Sadly, from all the articles that I can find, I think it seems safe to say that the Chain Lake Monster is folklore and nothing more.

Sources:

Rife, Philip L. *America's Loch Ness Monsters.* iUniverse, 2000.

Alexander Crawford Historical Society. "Pocomoonshine Lake Monster." [www.mainething.com/alexander/memories/POCOMOONSHINE%20LAKE%20MONSTER.htm]

"SNAIK STORIES"
FARMER KILLS STRANGE ANIMAL

FROM THE *Xenia Daily Gazette* of May 26, 1913:

FARMER KILLS A STRANGE ANIMAL

Samuel Chapman, a farmer near Pitchin, killed a strange animal in his ham yard Friday that has puzzled men familiar with wild animals. He was attracted by the quacking of a duck and went out to investigate, discovering the strange animal in the act of attacking the duck.

The animal ran into the barn at his approach but came back out and approached him with apparent friendliness. Surprised and somewhat alarmed by the strange appearance of the curiosity which confronted him, Mr. Chapman killed it with a club which he was carrying and took it to the house to look it over.

The animal, from its teeth, is a carnivorous one. It measured fourteen inches from the tip of its nose to the back of its tail and was covered with a thick fur, somewhat resembling a beaver's, shading from dark yellow near the base to a dark brown at the ends. The head was shaped somewhat like a mink's and the tail was about six inches long and furry.

Mr. Chapman has shown his catch to several persons well versed in natural history and even to an old trapper and hunter of the neighborhood all of whom declare, that the animal is strange to them.

14

A HAIRY WATER WHATSIT
"WHAT IS IT?" INDEED

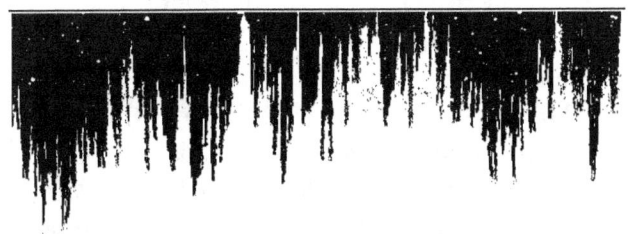

SIMILAR to the beast whose identity we puzzled over two chapters back, here we have yet another a mystery animal that just doesn't make sense. On December 8, 1885, the *Weekly Banner Watchman* out of Athens, Georgia, reported on the strange creature. All I can say is I wholeheartedly agree with the title of the article.

WHAT IS IT?

Strange Animal at Large Which has Terrorized a Neighborhood

Jackson (Ga.) News.

COWBOYS & SAURIANS

For some time past persons coming to this town from a westerly direction have reported seeing a strange animal, but just what it is no one has been able to determine. It has been variously described and discussed, and so many people only travel through the section of country west of here with fear and trepidation. The unknown animal is said by some to be as large as a mule, and when in pursuit or disturbed utters a piercing scream like unto that of whistle of a steam engine.

The beast readily takes to water, swims with marvelous rapidity, and at intervals, where the water is deep enough, dives beneath the waves out of sight and remains under for quite a time. The reports as to the appearance of the beast differ very much. One gentleman who claims he saw it at close range says it had a shaggy coating of hair, a large head, and ran with great speed. Another account states that while the animal sped through the water with amazing swiftness, when it came to the shoals its gate changed to a tumbling locomotion, similar to the progress of the seal.

Mr. Beauregard Heath, who lives near Flat Shoals, while walking along the Towaliga River recently was suddenly startled to see a strange monster shooting through the water, snorting and billowing in a manner that was appalling. The water where the creature was first seen by Mr. Heath was deep, but immediately ahead was quite a stretch of shoals, where the water was shallow. When the animal reached this portion

ICE AGE

of the river so great had its momentum grown that it shot upwards and out of the water, landing with a splash on its side. Then began its tumbling, pitching gate. Though it was a most awkward motion, it's speed was far greater than an ordinary fast walk. In less time than it takes to tell it, the amphibious animal was over the shoals, and with a shrill cry, disappeared in the deeper water beyond. When some 20 feet from where it shot into the water, it rose again, with a savage puff, and shaking the water from its huge head, went careening on its way. A bend in the stream hid it from Mr. Heath's gaze. In conversation, Mr. Heath said it was as large as a good-sized mule, and weighed he should judge, 600 or 700 pounds.

What has just been described is truly a strange creature. It would seem to be more at home in the water, not a trait of many quadruped mammals who are more suited for dry land. I wish the witnesses would have described the legs because it almost sounds as though it had flippers. But, surely, if it did, this strange detail would have been noted. One of the only odd, quadruped mammals that dwelled in the water was the Desmostylus, a hairy creature somewhat similar to a hippopotamus. The thing would have been clumsy on land, but also shouldn't have been terribly fast in the water as it mostly walked along the river bottoms.

As the creature is described as having an extra-large head, one Ice Age mammal that fits that description, and was about the height of a mule, was the Andrewsarchus of the Late Eocene period. However, I can find nothing to suggest that this animal was an adept swimmer.

A hairy, amphibious reptilian could also be a candidate. As such, perhaps a Cynodontia (a suborder of Therapsids) is in order? The cynodonts were essentially hairy, quadruped reptiles, and the best particular candidate for what was seen in Georgia was the cynognathus. Some cynodonts, like the Diademodon, were at one time theorized to have spent much time in lakes and streams like a hippo due to the examination of stable light isotopes of oxygen extracted from Diademodon fossils. Some scientists interpreted this to mean that the animals stayed in the water for long periods of time, though this idea has since been abandoned.

All that said, additional accounts from the article only further confuse as to what the animal could be.

> Other reputable gentlemen have seen it, and all are unanimous in saying they never saw anything which even resembled. None, however took the time to study its looks carefully, for when it presented an appearance they had urgent business in other quarters. [An African American man] saw it last week while out hunting. He was in the woods sneaking on a squirrel to get a shot, when, turning at the crackling of a branch, he saw behind him an animal, which he said looks like a lion, a bear and a monkey. Having no desire to post himself

ICE AGE

of any natural history – being no naturalist, and not caring to find out what beast family the uncanny thing actually belonged, he took a walk. As soon as he got the proper use of his limbs, he fairly flew through the woods – over stumps, through briars, across gullies, until he struck the dirt road, and was home. A news report asked to the Negro about the circumstances yesterday, and further asked him to describe the animal's looks. "I never stops to examine him closely. Just as I was making up my mind to look at it, it showed its teeth and I left in a hurry."

To interrupt again, I think that it's important to note that since the man didn't see this creature in the water, it could've been a different cryptid entirely from the one described earlier. Notably, he mentions nothing about it having clumsy movements on land. And, I can find no animal that looks like a cross between a lion, a bear, and a monkey. I can only presume that he meant to imply the creature perhaps had either a mane like a lion or a feline face on the body of a bear. As to the monkey and the lion both, I would assume the beast had a tail. If anything, its closest match might be the Sarkastodon. To return to the article...

Mr. OS Williams, who came into town yesterday, when crossing the Towaliga River, saw a strange-looking object swimming in the river some distance away from him. He could not determine what it was, having never seen anything resembling it. On his way to town he met Mr. Willis Evans, accompanied by several other parties, who stated to him that they were going in quest of the unknown beast which had been terrorizing the people along the Towaliga river. Mr. Williamson recalled to mind the strange creature he had seen swimming the river, and he spoke to the party about it. Breathlessly they informed him that that was what they were in quest of, and leaving him they hurried on towards the river. The result of their hunt will be anxiously looked for, and it is to be hoped that they will be successful.

What sort of beast it is no one can even conjecture. It is possible that it is some animal which is escaped from a strolling menagerie, and though a stranger in a strange land, has managed to live and thrive. The News will keep its readers posted, and if the unknown creature is captured our readers will be fully appraised of the event, together with the most minute particulars pertaining thereto.

In summary, it's nearly impossible to narrow it down to just one candidate for what this creature was. It may not have even been a survivor from prehistoric times and may have simply been a heretofore unknown animal that remains undiscovered to this day.

15
THE DOG EATER
A CRUEL KENTUCKY CRYPTID

IN THE WORLD of Fortean investigation, there is such a thing as a "flap of sightings." This refers to a relatively short period of time—in the greater scheme of history—wherein a particular phenomenon, cryptid, or being is observed. It could be for a few weeks, months, or even years. But the point is it has a beginning and an end, and in many cases, the mystery creature is never seen again, unlike Bigfoot and the Loch Ness Monster, consistent in their appearances.

Spring-Heeled Jack is a good example. The strange being terrorized London in the late 1830s for a little over a year and was never seen again. Naturally, the description differed depending upon the witness, but fundamentally Spring-Heeled Jack had the shape and appearance of a man. Sometimes the man was tall and thin, other times stocky and burly. Some reports had him wearing a cape with a lamp on his chest, others said he had wings—a few even said that he breathed fire. The common denominator was always that the man-thing could jump significant distances, hence the name Spring-Heeled Jack.[38] I use this example to illustrate that even though people were seeing the same being, each had a different interpretation of it—and to a degree, the same will be true of the creature we are about to discuss in this chapter.

For several years denizens in the vicinity of Danville, Kentucky were terrorized by a creature that they dubbed the "dog eater." The reign of terror began in 1885 and continued sporadically into the 1890s. Like so many monsters before it, the "dog eater" was given a myriad of different characteristics and traits. A consistent behavior the beast exhibited was tearing off the heads of animals and leaving the bodies behind. An odd, one-off trait it once exhibited was draining the blood of its prey and not eating the body. In terms of description, it was a quadrupedal mammal. Its size would vary, as is to be expected, and witnesses could never seem to make up their mind as to whether it was a panther, a huge dog, or even a bear.

---

[38] In the interest of being thorough, beings similar to Spring-Heeled Jack pop up from time to time. But their sightings are not well documented or as frequent as the original case.

ICE AGE

The first article that I found on the beast was published in the April 7, 1885 edition of the *Hopkinsville Semi Weekly South Kentuckian* on the front page.[39] As you'll see within the first few sentences, witnesses were certainly not in agreement as to what they were seeing.

The "Dog Eater."

The sensation of the day is the so-called Dog Eater. That an animal of some sort has been roaming about the country, and that it has killed a number of dogs, is sufficiently established. As to the description of the animal accounts differ very widely. Some say it looks like a lion, others think it more like a bengal tiger, another that it is like an alligator. The preponderance of the evidence, however, seems to be to the effect that it is black, and differing from a large Newfoundland dog mostly by its great length. It first attracted attention in the western part of Boyle, migrated to the eastern part of Marion, went back to Boyle, and was heard from last week in Washington County. The mystery surrounding the nature and movements of the beast soon fired the popular imagination, and upon the few facts known about it here has sprung up a vast and fantastic mythology.

---

[39] If that name strikes a chord in your memory, you're probably thinking of the Hopkinsville Goblins that attacked a farm house in Kentucky in the 1950s.

Only three days later, the *Stanford Semi Weekly Interior Journal* ran another story about how a local man, Henry Owens, had been stalked by the beast as he walked to town. The same paper reported on June 17, 1887, that a strange animal had been seen on the farm of Roy Arnold. The man's son saw the beast and described it as being yellow in color, three feet long, and having a bushy tail. Despite only being three feet long, he claimed that its teeth were 12 inches!

Our next mention of the beast comes from this article three years later from the *Columbus Enquirer* on November 23, 1888:

The greatest sensation of Jasper county now is created by what is called a dog eater. It goes at night to different houses, and wherever it finds a small dog, or one it can easily conquer, it kills it and eats its head off. No one knows what the thing is, and there is considerable excitement over it.

Though it was supposedly seen off and on for the next several years, I can find no other account of it until the *Cincinnati Commercial Gazette* published the following on July 20, 1891, on page 2:

A DOG DESTROYER.

A Mysterious Monster That Is Rapidly Reducing the Canine Population of Casey County, Ky.

ICE AGE

Danville, Ky., July 19.—[Special.]—The peaceful residents in the vicinity of the village of Dunnville, in Casey County, are just now very much exercised and nonplussed by the appearance of a strange and destructive animal in their neighborhood, and which, for the want of a better appellation, they term "the dog-eater." Some three years ago the people of the west end of this county were the victims of the depredations of a similar animal, and the name of "the dog-eater" was given it because it preyed upon the canine tribe exclusively, and seemingly having an appetite for no other game. He suddenly disappeared from that section, however, much to the relief of the inhabitants and the local newspapers, and it was hoped that his absence would be permanent. But the animal is now creating the furore in Casey County, which is comparatively only a short distance from the scene of the former trouble, must be the original "dog-eater." The first indication of his return was last Tuesday night, or Wednesday morning rather, when Mr. G. R. Williams, who owns a large pack of fox hounds, went out to where the dogs had been chained the night before and found every one of them stark dead. There was very little evidence of a struggle, and for quite a while Mr. Williams could form no idea of the manner in which his dogs met their death.

After a second and more careful examination he found that each dog had a small wound in the throat, and he soon saw that whatever did the work overpowered the poor brutes with very little difficulty, and then perforating their throats, sucked their life blood. The report of the affair soon spread abroad, and large numbers of the neighbors came in during the day to view the work of destruction, a great many of them thought it the work of a panther, or "painter," as the backwoodsmen term those ferocious beasts, but this could not be, as the panther feeds upon the entire carcass. Hunting parties were formed, as had been two years before in the Perryville neighborhood, but with the same futile results. Not being able to ascertain its hiding place, the country folks decided to endeavor to lure the mysterious visitor to the scene of Tuesday night slaughter, and they accordingly secured a worthless cur and tied it in a place convenient for watching the proceedings. A party of the farmers, heavily armed, hid in ambush Thursday night and patiently awaited the appearance of "the dog-eater." Through the long hours of the night they watched. Twelve, 1 and 2 o'clock came, and no dog-eater broke the silence. Just as the sentries were about to give up, however, a whine was heard, and they looked in the direction of the imprisoned cur, and the sight that met their gaze almost froze the blood in their veins.

The moon was shining brightly, and over the crouching form of the decoy dog they saw an immense white animal, unlike any other they had ever seen. They say it was built upon the greyhound pattern, but larger in every way, being four feet high and about six feet from the end of its tail to the tip of its nose or snout. So interested and frightened were they that not a gun was fired, and after the strange beast had finished its meal it calmly galloped away. The men went to the dead dog and found that it had been wounded in the same way as the hounds killed two nights before.

This is undoubtedly the same animal seen in the west end of this county two years ago. It was then seen by various parties, and the description they gave tallies with the one given above. One gentleman, who saw it attack a dog, says when the dog saw the "dog-eater" it was overcome with terror and seemed to be unable to move or to defend itself, and fell an easy victim to the enemy. The tracks left by the animal are similar to those made by a bird, though of course magnified many times, and showing that it has powerful talons.

Some rather wild details are given in this article, notably that the animal drank blood. Back then, the Chupacabra was not a part of American folklore, nor does the animal sighted seem to match such a creature's description. That they compare the tracks to those made by a bird is truly bizarre. It should be noted that this was the only instance where the "dog eater" drank blood. Perhaps this was a different creature altogether that was given the same moniker by mistake?

Whatever the case, by 1892, the dog eater had traveled south down to nearby Tennessee. The *Brownsville Daily Herald* out of Texas reported on the beast's depredations there in its December 28, 1892 edition. The story reported how the area was in a furor over the beast, which had a nasty habit of decapitating dogs! Locals described it as looking like a calf with fetters (chains) attached to its neck. Like so many articles of the time, it concluded by supposing that it was an escaped circus animal, in this case, a panther.

The following article appeared in the *Evening Times* out of Monroe, Wisconsin, on October 28, 1893:

A MONSTROUS BRUTE

Nothing Like It Known To The Most Eminent Zoologists

It Has a Broad Body, Flat Head, Big Fiery Eyes, Woolly Hide, Bushy Tail, Powerful Limbs and Bleeding Mouth.

The "dog eater," panther, or whatever it is that has created consternation time and again throughout the section among the country folks, has again made its appearance, after an interval of something like a year, says a Danville (Ky.) dispatch to the Cincinnati Enquirer. The existence of the strange animal has been scoffed at by the skeptics, but persons of undoubted veracity who claim to have seen the monster during its midnight prowling say they are willing to make oath to the statements concerning it.

ICE AGE

About five years ago it made its appearance in this country and several parties were organized in the vicinity of Perryville to hunt the strange beast down and exterminate it, but none were successful in their mission. From the fact that it seldom, if ever, attacked anything save dogs, the people gave it the name of the "dog eater," and by this it has been known for about seven years. Persons versed in natural history say they can recall nothing like it, and seem to think, from the descriptions given by those who have caught glimpses of the animal, that it is a cross between a panther and a mastiff, though the descriptions vary so at times that such a conclusion cannot be relied upon.

Its last appearance was in Mercer County, a short distance from the city. James O'Connor and the colored driver of R.E. Coleman's bus were returning from Burgin with several passengers aboard, and had just passed the old Walden farm and were coming downhill at a moderately rapid gate, when suddenly the team stopped, reared, snorted and plunged about, almost upsetting the bus and badly frightening the passengers, acting just as horses have been seen to do when scared by some strange beast.

In a moment the occupants of the vehicle were startled and almost paralyzed at seeing an animal of enormous size and ferocious looks spring out of the woodland into the road, glare at the conveyance a moment and then leisurely leave the scene without molesting anything. The animal was distinctly seen by Mr. O'Connor and the driver, who were sitting upon the front seat. They describe it as being of a dark color, with a broad, flat like body and head, large, fiery eyes, woolly hide, powerful limbs, bushy tail and a monstrous head and mouth. There can be no doubt of Mr. O'Connor having seen this animal, as he would not concoct such a strange story, and his testimony about the appearance of the beast is corroborated by others who have seen it.

The question asked many by is: what is this monster that comes and goes, and still molests nothing except the worthless curs of the country, except now and then destroying a fancy setter? It is no stranger in Mercer County. Several years back there was a current report that some strange animal had taken up its abode in Boone's cave, and the people there about, especially the colored portion, were very much alarmed, and afraid to venture out after night. A few determined ones, however, explored the cave, but failed to find the monster, though they discovered strange looking tracks in the moist earth on the floor of the cave.

...

A year or so after this several parties in the vicinity of Burgin claim to have seen this nocturnal visitor, and numerous dead dogs, some almost completely devoured and others scarcely touched, attested to the existence of some fell destroyer. After a career of about three months in that vicinity the monster was next heard of in Casey county, where it

ICE AGE

appeared one night and destroyed twelve fine hound dogs belonging to a hunter living near Dunnville. The owner of these dogs concluded he would kill the pestiferous animal, and so he tied a dog to a stake and awaited its return on another night. While watching for the beast he fell asleep, and toward midnight he was awakened by the yelp of the dog he had tied, he jumped to his feet, gun in hand, just in time to see the game he was after disappearing over the hill, the dog's head having been bitten off. This was the last time the strange animal was seen in Casey county.

...

Mr. Woodford G. Portwood, of this city, says he plainly saw the dog-eater one night while he was with a fishing party on Dick's river. Mr. Portwood was some distance from camp, unaccompanied, save by his valuable pointer dog Jeff, that follows him wherever he goes. He was attending to a number of poles which he had set for catfish, and Jeff had wandered up the river some distance, when Mr. Portwood was attracted by a commotion in the bushes, accompanied by loud grunts and the howling of his dog Jeff. Directly the dog came rapidly running toward him, followed by a ferocious looking beast, which stopped as soon as it had seen the owner of the dog, looked at Mr. Portwood a moment, its eyes like two burning balls of fire, turned and went back into the bushes. The dog was trembling like a leaf, and has never been induced to go back to that particular spot of the river since. Colonel Thorp Shaw, who was in the camp that night, corroborates Mr. Portwood's story to the extent that he also heard the loud howling of the dog and that Portwood immediately left the catfish poles to take care of themselves until morning.

Two other gentlemen, Mr. Phil Marks and Edward H. Fox, the artist, claimed to have seen this remarkable beast one night as they were returning from a coon hunting expedition. They were riding leisurely along the pike, engaged in conversation, their fine pack of hounds following behind, wary and worn out after the chase, when suddenly Mark's horse reared up and had it not been for Mr. Marx's expert horsemanship he would have been thrown backward against the ground. Mr. Fox, who preserved his presence of mind, soon saw the cause of the trouble. The dog eater had stepped out into the road ahead of the party and began drinking out of a small stream, and right here this animal's strange influence over dogs was illustrated. The hounds following along seemed to become paralyzed with fright. They huddled together trembling with fear and whining piteously. Mr. Fox drew his revolver and shot at the dog eater, which jumped over the fence and disappeared. The artist is confident that he hit the monster, but thinks that the thick coating of hair on it was too much for the small bullet used. After the animal had got out of the way the hounds struck for home at a 2:40 gait. Mr. Marx can be found at his place of business in the city

ICE AGE

at any time, and will cheerfully detail the story of his experience with the now noted animal. Mr. Fox, at the request of the reporter, made a rough sketch of the dog eater as it appeared to him.

THAT MOST WONDERFUL ANIMAL.

ILLUSTRATION BY FOX.

Considering that Fox was an artist, I suppose we should consider his sketch to be an accurate representation of the creature. For if it were a normal mountain lion or panther, would he not draw it as such? The critter pictured above doesn't look like any cat I've ever seen, and Fox also gave it webbed feet. This would seem to corroborate the statements in the 1891 article about the beast's footprints: "The tracks left by the animal are similar to those made by a bird, though of course magnified many times, and showing that it has powerful talons."

CHARLES KNIGHT'S DEPICTION OF A BORHYAENA, FAR RIGHT.

If one were to propose a prehistoric animal as the candidate, I might start with a Borhyaena, which lived during the late Oligocene into the early Miocene. It was about five feet long, which I must admit is not what one might describe as an "animal of enormous size" as one witness once did. However, a previous report described the animal as six feet long, close in size to what a Borhyaena was thought to be. Furthermore, the Borhyaena was a type of marsupial, which often had webbed feet. This again gels with the 1891 article that reported it left clawed footprints like a bird. The animal was carnivorous and was one of the primary predators of its day. The head was bear-like and the tail long and bushy. (I also considered a Thylacoleo

ICE AGE

as a candidate. However, it had prominent, beaver-like front incisors, while Mr. Fox's drawing did not and had fangs.)

Whatever it was, it's possible that the "dog eater" was killed in 1893. However, its description is somewhat more mundane and certainly doesn't seem to match Mr. Fox's drawing. The story was reported in the *Cincinnati Commercial Gazette* on November 26, 1893, on page 10:

THE DOG EATER.
Peculiar, Animal the Terror of Farmers, Killed In Kentucky.

Harrodsburg, Ky., November 25.—(Special.)— For several years a strange animal has infested this locality. Taking Harrodsburg as a center, this peculiar quadruped has been seen within a radius of ten miles at different times and places. Between High Bridge and Burgen, two years since, the natives were afraid to venture out of doors after dark lest they would encounter the dog-eater, as he was familiarly called. He was said to be a regular "Jack the Ripper" on dogs especially, killing every dog that chanced to come in his way. No dog could be made to encounter this ferocious animal. Many incredulous stories were circulated in regard to the different times the dog-eater was seen, and the number of canines he had destroyed.

A few months ago a vehicle loaded with passengers was being drawn to Harrodsburg when the docile team took fright at a strange, peculiar arrival that crossed the road, and a catastrophy narrowly averted. All parties concerned agreed that this was a visitation of the veritable dog-eater.

Yesterday there was a report current on the street that the dog-eater had been killed and that his skin was to be seen at a saloon. Hundreds went to see it. There it was, in the back room, on exhibition, the hide of the notorious dog-eater. It was about eight feet long from end of nose to tip of tail and from two to four feet in height. This dog-eater was shot the day before in the vicinity of Perryville, ten miles from this place. He had massacred several dogs and was making said havoc in a flock of sheep when a farmer named Taylor shot him with a load of buck-shot.

This animal was no doubt a cross between a she wolf and a Newfoundland dog. Still many claim it is of a species purely its own, and is the dog-eater, and nothing else.

There is a range of low, rocky hills that traverse this State, called "The Knobs," that are distant not more than three or four miles from Perryvllle, where this strange creature was killed. Some years since a wolf was killed in this locality; and as it was a male, the female was supposed to have been left to roam the hills by herself. This mongrel that had been killed was a terror to children and colored people of all ages.

ICE AGE

This strange animal had been frequently seen in the vicinity of Perryville, and is said to have galloped instead of being able to run like a dog.[40]

And thus ends the saga of the "Dog Eater." After this article, I found no mention of it ever again—though the name "dog eater" was certainly given to other mystery animals across the U.S. before and after this. But, the Kentucky "Dog Eater" did not resurface. I think in all likelihood the "Dog Eater" was multiple animals often blamed for the same killings. I do think that one of them, however, was exceptional, and was indeed the primary "Dog Eater." Whatever it was, it warrants a more thorough investigation by someone more knowledgeable than myself.

---

[40] This galloping motion was also described in the 1891 article.

"SNAIK STORIES"
OGOPOGO'S OBITUARY

☞ SADLY, Canada's most famed cryptid outside of the Sasquatch, Ogopogo, died sometime around December 29, 1926, according to the associate press:

LAKE OKANOGAN'S MONSTER IS DEAD FROZEN UNDER ICE

VANCOUVER, Dec. 29.— Ogopogo, sheep-headed monster of Okanogan Lake, which startled a score of Lake residents last summer, is dead, a victim of cold weather, the Morning Star reported today. It was frozen under by ice, which thinly covered the lake.

Peter Simon, half breed Indian of Kelowna, British Columbia, thus told of the death struggle, which he alone saw from behind a tree.

"Heaving, cracking ice torn asunder by some monstrous struggle, and thrown into mounds on the shore," said Simon, "the giant form, sinuous and powerful, the tail thrashing for freedom and the huge head bearing a ghastly resemblance to a sheep."

After seeing this, Peter crept cautiously to the shore, assured himself that the monster was dead, dropped his rifle and ran for home.

Calgary newspaper men who investigated descriptions of the reported monster, declared it probably was an or fish or ribbonfish. If anything. He or fish, a deep sea monster, has been a source of sea serpent stories on the north Atlantic coast for centuries. It has a pronounced sheeplike head, is 15 to 20 feet long and from 10 to 12 inches deep with a continuous dorsal fin.

16
WHAT WAS THE WAHHOO
ANOTHER SHUNKA WARAK'IN?

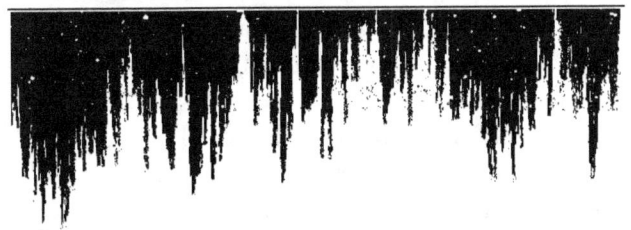

LATE 1870S NEVADA was the location of a flap of sightings of a cryptid dubbed alternatively as the Wahhoo and the Whoahaw. The beast was similar in size and description to the Shunka Warak'in. Some cryptozoologists (notably David Weatherly) think it may have even been of the same species. As such, the Whoahaw/Wahhoo might well be another Borophagus, a hyena-like dog from the Pleistocene epoch.

The animal was first reported in Nevada in the *Reno Gazette-Journal* on August 26, 1879, on page three:

THE WHOAHAW.
—
A Hunting Party's Experience — The Strange Creature that Dominates Deeth — Stories of

COWBOYS & SAURIANS

His Ferocity— Abundance of Game and Good Sport.

Richard Smith, the express agent, and his brother H. R., got back last Sunday night from their hunting expedition. They shot over the country around about Deeth and Halleck. Game was abundant. During the trip they bagged 125 prairie chickens and one lynx, besides untold numbers of sage hens, rabbits, ducks, etc. The singular number of lynx shot by the party would appear to indicate a scarcity of large game in that section of the state explored by the expedition. One might suppose that where birds were so abundant, lynx and other of their four footed enemies would be more numerous. It is a striking fact that they killed only one of the carnivora during the trip. But there is an explanation for the scarcity of such animals that will be strange to many readers. The whole region round about Deeth is dominated by

A MYSTERIOUS BEAST known locally as the Whoahaw, an animal supposed to be a cross between the grizzly bear and the coyote. As the mule combines all the bad qualities of the horse and the ass, so does this hybrid display the courage and ferocity of the grizzly joined to the cunning and treachery of the coyote. The whoahaw has never been seen by daylight. He roams and ravages only at night. The beast has been known to carry off a horse. Cattle and sheep are often borne away by the monster. Mules he never attacks, for some unexplained reason. The brothers often sat up far into the night listening to the ranchmen's tales of the strength and ferocity of the whoahaw. There is supposed to be only one of them in that section of the country, he has never been distinctly seen, but some of the ranchers have caught glimpses of him prowling about in the darkness. They always had business of importance to attend to somewhere else upon such occasions. The recital of tales about the fearful creature one night,

CURDLED THE BLOOD of H. R. Smith almost to coagulation. Richard says the ranchmen's stories often ran his own circulation down from seventy to forty beats a minute. Nothing but the speedy administration of tea or other stimulant could have enabled them to pull through those narratives. The brothers camped in the vicinity several nights, almost daring to hope that they might catch a glimpse of the dangerous hybrid. But they saw nothing of him, although one midnight they heard far off an echoing sound like "whoa-----haw," which the ranchmen said was the cry of the monster, and from which they gave him his name. Should some adventurous hunter eventually cope with and kill the curious beast it is to be hoped for the sake of science, that, his bones and skin will be carefully preserved. The brothers did not meet with any exciting adventures during their trip. They were much impressed with exceeding swiftness of the coyote, when stimulated to exertion by the presence of fine shot under the skin. In order to observe his velocity they frequently introduced fine shot under the hide of strugglin' coyotes, always with the most gratifying results. They recommend the neighborhood of Deeth for hunting, but "Beware," they say, "of the whoahaw."

On August 29th, the monster was sighted again outside a home in Reno. This time it was called the Wahhoo in the article printed in the *Reno Gazette-Journal* on September 4, 1879:

Was It A Wahhoo?

A. A. Adams is a well-known and highly respected German citizen. His residence is near the corner of Fourth and Chestnut streets. Mr. Adams is a bachelor, and lives in a small cottage [in Reno]. He is not superstitious, and never clouds his mind with ardent spirits. ... So when he heard some heavy animal walking slowly up and down his verandah last Friday night [August 29], he did not suppose that the noises were in any way supernatural. He simply wondered what kind of a beast could have got into his yard. He listened, and could distinctly hear the tread of some four-footed creature, as it slowly trod to and fro. He could even hear the scratch of the creatures claws on the boards. His curiosity at

ICE AGE

length aroused, Mr. Adams determined to take a look at the pedestrian on his portico.

He rose from his bed, and, putting on an additional garment, he stepped forth into the rheumy and unpurged air of midnight. The moon was shining from a cloudless sky, and by its sight seemed a large black bulldog. The animal stopped in its walk, and turned two brilliant, fiery eyes upon Mr. Adams. They glowed with an unnatural brightness; looking more like hot coals than visual organs. He noticed, too, that its 'snoot' was very long, like a pig's; and its tail of surprising length, stuck straight out behind. Mr. Adams clearly saw that, whatever his strange visitor might be, it was no bulldog. After looking at him steadily for over a minute, the beast slowly retreated to the fence, which it climbed by means of its claws, after the manner of a cat. Perched upon the top of the fence, the creature sat, and resumed its survey of the astonished German. Mr. Adams thought he would direct a stream of water from the garden hose upon the animal, and thereby induce it to retire. He did so, but, to his amazement, the creature remained immovable, merely presenting its snout to the stream, its body enveloped in a cloud of spray. Mr. Adams persevered in the hydropathic treatment for about ten minutes, but still the beast kept its position, its eyes glaring at him like the red lights of a railway train.

Mr. Adams owns to a feeling of dread at the creatures peculiar persistence under the circumstances, and began to think that ghost stories might be true after all. He retreated into the house and locked the door. He looked out of the window, and there still sat the animal on the top of the fence, its baleful eyes throwing a lurid glare into the room. Mr. Adams now felt a great fall in the temperature. He was shivering with cold. He thought he would fire a charge of shot at the brute, and got out his gun for the purpose. He loaded the weapon hastily, but after he had put on the caps, concluded he wouldn't fire after all. He pulled down the blinds, and went back to bed.

He listened for a long time, but heard no more footsteps. The cold continued, and Mr. Adams shivered nearly all night, and got very little rest in consequence. At daylight next morning he was out, and made a careful search of the yard, closely examined the fence and porch, but discovered no trace of the strange beast. He put his gun in careful order, and made up his mind that should the creature come again he would fire upon it at sight. He was surprised to find, on cleaning the weapon, that in loading it the night before, he had put the shot in first, and the powder afterward....

Mr. Adams carefully loaded the gun that day, putting in the powder first to avoid the mistakes apt to attend that operation when performed in the dark. The following night he sat up late in company, with a countryman of his, but saw nothing unusual, nor has he since been visited by the mysterious beast. No animal answering to

ICE AGE

the description is known to exist in this section of the country.

In addition to the peculiarities already described, Mr. Adams said it had a long, slender neck. Could it have been one of those ferocious hybrids called wahhoos, which are said to prowl at night in the neighborhood of Halleck and Deeth?... The mystery may yet be cleared up, but now the question is, among many who hear the story, was it a wahhoo?"

Stories of the animal continued to pour in, such as this one on September 9, 1879, from the *Reno Evening Gazette*:

Wahhoo, or What?

A strange looking animal was seen by two sportsmen on the road about two miles from Peavine last Sunday. This creature was not unlike a coyote but larger, yet too small for a bear. It was running on the side of a hill with wonderful speed, and disappeared in a moment. Could the beast have been a Wahhoo?"

And then, only three days later in the same paper, this story:

The Wild Wahhoo!
A "Man-Eater" that opens the Graves of the Dead. A Full Description of the Strange Beast—Its Pedal Peculiarities—Its Haunts in the Hills—

COWBOYS & SAURIANS

Found in Nevada, Idaho and Montana—A Creature with the Form of a Dog and the Voice of a Jackass.

THE WILD WAHHOO!

A "Man-Eater" that Opens the Graves of the Dead.

A Full Description of the Strange Beast— Its Pedal Peculiarities — Its Haunts in the Hills—Found in Nevada, Idaho and Montana—A Creature with the Form of a Dog and the Voice of a Jackass.

RENO EVENING GAZETTE 9-12-79

A recent number of the Gazette contained some account of an animal found in the neighborhood of Halleck and Deeth, Nevada, known in that section of country as the "Wahhoo." It appears that the creature is not known to naturalists and finds no place in the catalogs of writers upon zoology. Some readers of the article referred to for this reason supposed the whole story to be a hoax. But it must be remembered that every day the researches of scientists are bringing to light hitherto unknown animals and plants, in every quarter of the globe. Animals well-known locally, in some remote localities of the earth, often prove entirely new and strange to the world of science. The narratives of travelers are often received with a great deal of incredulity because they frequently contain descriptions of things before unheard of. When Du Chaillu discovered the gorilla in Africa, scientists were slow to believe in the existence of the animal. Nearer home there is a fish in Idaho called the "redfish," which is familiar to the people of that territory, yet has never been scientifically described, and of which no specimen has yet been placed in the Smithsonian Institute.

The account of the Wahhoo which follows is plain and unvarnished, and it may yet be found that this strange beast will possess a high scientific interest to workers in the field of natural history. In the brief and imperfect description of the Wahhoo to which reference has already been made, were given some data relating to the animal, which were furnished by Richard Smith, the agent of Wells, Fargo & Co.'s express, at Reno.

That gentleman, while hunting in the neighborhood of Halleck, heard from residents of that locality many stories of the Wahhoo and its peculiarities. He did not succeed in catching a glimpse of one, but his brother who was with him succeeded in obtaining the dressed hide of a Wahhoo and took it with him to Los Angeles on his return from the expedition. Mr. Smith's Reno friends, to whom he repeated some of the stories he had heard of the strange creature, were skeptical of their truth. But the publication of the article in the Gazette brought to light some additional testimony concerning the curious beast. Before proceeding with an entirely new evidence, it will be well to state what the people about Deeth say of the animal. It is they who are known both as the Wahhoo and the maneater.

The former appellation is supposed to have been given it in imitation of the peculiar noise it makes. The latter designation originated in the known propensity of the beast to dig up and devour bodies of the dead. Wahhoos which have been killed near Deeth exhibit a peculiar structure. The legs are short, and the paws very large proportionally, furnished with strong projecting claws of great length. This formation enables the creature to dig with ease and rapidity. The body is long and slender, the tail of medium length and usually curved over the back, the neck short, the head broad, and the jaws provided with formidable teeth. The skin is covered with long, fine hair. Its prevailing color is black, spotted with white. In weight it varies from fifty to seventy-five pounds. The creature is larger than a coyote, and in appearance, when seen at a distance, not unlike a large dog. In conversation with Mr. Smith, a young man said that he had shot a number of Wahhoos, that he carefully measured each specimen, and found that the left legs of each were somewhat shorter than the right legs. Although his informant persisted in the assertion, a statement must be regarded with great caution.

ICE AGE

The probability is that he measured a malformed specimen and jumped to the conclusion that the others showed the same peculiarities. The young man stated, as an explanation for the inequality in the length of the creature's legs, that the Wahhoo was found only upon the hills, along the sides of which it was constantly traveling. The unequal length of its legs would be advantageous to the animal in traversing the hillsides. It would indeed be strange if nature had provided such a marvelous adaptation of structure to fit the creature for ranging upon the sides of hills. Incredible as such a statement certainly is, it might possibly be true. Knowing in what strange forms of life have inhabited the earth in bygone epochs, nothing seems impossible in animated nature. In the presence of the fossil remains of the Eohippus, or fivetoed horse, a laterally unequal wahhoo would not seem so strange a creature after all.

Daniel Roberts, an express messenger on the Central Pacific Railroad, states that in Montana wahhoos are not uncommon. He saw and heard the creature in Idaho in 1867. He has vivid recollection of his first sight of one of the beasts. He was approaching a station in Beaver canyon, one evening in the summer of that year, after a long journey on horseback. On the way up the canyon he heard what he supposed was the bray of a mule. He remarked to his companion, who was familiar with the country, that they must be near the camp. He was told that the noise was made by a wahhoo, and shortly afterward they saw the animal sitting on its haunches above them and giving utterance to the dismal cry, which had deceived Mr. Roberts. The creature walked along the edge of the precipice for some distance, at intervals sitting upon its haunches and sending forth its prolonged, wailing bay.

A man named Thomas, well-known to Mr. Roberts, shortly after killed a wahhoo on the Montana road, near the Camas Creek station. It weighed about seventy pounds and fought wickedly after being wounded, until it was finally dispatched. Not long after that, Mr. Roberts, in company with Mr. Bassett, a superintendent in the employ of the Western Union telegraph company, saw two wahhoos together near a place called Summit Station. He states that the animal is well-known all over Montana. It is very shy, nocturnal in its habits, and abides in the wilderness away from the habitations of men. It is going to these reasons that so little is yet known of the wahhoo. The foregoing meager description is all that the Gazette has been able to learn of the mysterious beast. It is published in the hope that the attention of some zoologist may be drawn to the fact of the existence of such a creature, and that the animal may prove a subject for the study and investigation of someone qualified to classify and describe it. All communications designed to throw any light upon the nature and habits of the wahhoo will be gratefully acknowledged.

ICE AGE

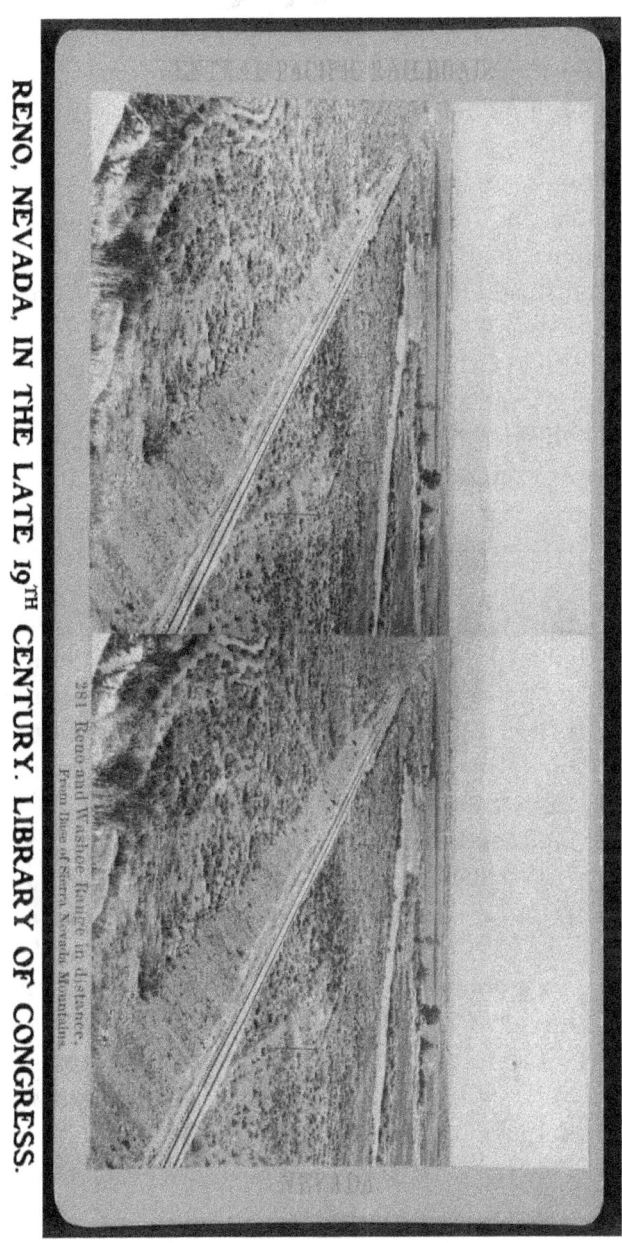

RENO, NEVADA, IN THE LATE 19ᵀᴴ CENTURY. LIBRARY OF CONGRESS.

COWBOYS & SAURIANS

This was, in my opinion, the last legitimate article on the Wahhoo, as the next two I found were satiric in nature. I attribute this in part to the odd belief that the animal was lopsided, with longer legs on the right side (I think the paper's speculation that Smith measured a malformed specimen was more likely). This odd trait would humorously be attributed to the animals in the last article to cover them at the time.

Our next sighting was reported five days after the previous article in the *Weekly Reno Gazette* published on September the 18th (though the letter was written on the 17th):

A Wahhoo Seen Near Wadsworth — A Party in Pursuit.

Ed. Gazette:—Report was brought to town yesterday that a wahhoo bad been seen in the mountains west of town. The night before, the people of Jones' ranch had been aroused by the wahhoo's long-drawn howl, which was likened to a shrill fog-whistle. They saw the mountains illumined as with an electric light.

This they found was owing to the glare of the creature's eyeballs. It sat upon a neighboring cliff, and so brilliant was the light emitted that none could gaze upon the creature, even for an instant.

This report, backed by authority, so excited our nimrods that a hunt was organized immediately. Jake Lewis, J. W. Holbrook, Wm. Pierson and others started this morning, and

ICE AGE

brilliant work is looked for before the close of day.

Anticipating that a lengthened hunt might prove necessary, the party laid in provisions, of which the following is a summary: Whiskey, 200 rounds ammunition, demijohn, 1 piece bacon, limes, 1 bottle whiskey, 1 box cigars, 50 rounds additional whiskey, more whiskey.

The result of the chase is awaited with breathless anxiety. A special reporter accompanied the party, and full particulars will be given on their return.   Subscriber.
Wadsworth, Sept. 17, 1870.

As you can tell from the supplies that included whiskey and more whiskey, this article was poking fun at the sighting, if it even happened. The likelihood that the animal's eyes were bright enough to cause a person to look away was also unlikely and seemed to be a spoof of earlier articles that described the animal's eyes. I could find no more reports on the animal from 1879. The next article was published in the *Reno Evening Gazette* on January 8, 1880. As it turned out, it would tell of the Wahoo pack's final stand...

Totally Extinct
Waylaying the Wahoo on a Mountain Side
The Last of These Strange Animals.

The cold weather is said to have killed off all the wahoos about Halleck and Deeth. A Wells-Fargo messenger reports that on last Saturday morning a party of Deeth hunters found wahoo tracks in the snow five miles northeast of the station. The severity of the weather appeared to have forced the animals to band together, as the tracks could not have been made by less than six different animals.

The circumstance excited the interest of the hunters, for anyone who knows what a wahoo is, knows full well that the creature is one of the most unsocial of all animated beings. The hunters determined to follow up the broad trail made by the wahoos, and at once started in pursuit. The tracks led them around the base of a high mountain and constantly ascended in a continuous spiral. The hunters followed the trail for hours, constantly climbing higher and higher, until at length the summit was reached, and the trail began to wind back down the mountain.

The hunters were now thoroughly exasperated and pressed on with fierce determination. The chase went on for hours until they reached the plain again and found that the wahoo's track had some proposed to give up the pursuit, but one of the party said if they would follow him they would fix the wahoos. He reminded them that owing to the fact that the wahoos' left legs are shorter than its right, the creature always walks on the hillside from right to left. His proposal was that that hunters should ascend the hill in the opposite way, and thus head off the wahoos and take them at a disadvantage.

ICE AGE

PREHISTORIC BOROPHAGUS.

So with fresh enthusiasm the party started off again, and after an hours' climb they met six wahoos face to face, halfway up the summit. Three of the creatures fell at the first fire. The others tried to turn and run but owing to their legs being shorter on one side than on the other they immediately lost their balance and rolled helplessly to the bottom of the slope, where the hunters subsequently found their lifeless carcasses.

This little band of devoted wahoos probably was the last of these curious animals. The few others that roamed the hills in the vicinity of Deeth and Halleck are believed to have perished in the late cold snap, and thus the wahoo, like the dodo, may at last be considered extinct.

Again, I find this story somewhat troubling because I feel it is folkloric more than anything else. The detail about the right and left legs, as I stated earlier, is carried over into this story from a previous article. However, we shall not let the last two articles destroy the credibility of the Wahhoo.

The Wahhoo's saving grace may well be the previous article published on September 12, 1879, in the *Reno Evening Gazette*. That article told how the Wahhoo had also been seen in Idaho and Montana, which lines up with what we learned in Chapter 8. As you'll no doubt remember, Israel Hutchins shot one of the creatures in Montana, though this was never reported in the local papers that I know of. That this article recounts additional sightings in Montana bolsters not only the Ringdocus sightings, in which a body was preserved, but also the Wahhoo sightings. After all, since we have concrete proof that the Ringdocus/Shunka Warak'in was real, why then couldn't the Wahhoo have existed as well?

Sources:

Weatherly, David. *Silver State Monsters: Cryptids and Legends of Arizona*. Nevada: Leprechaun Press, 2019.

"SNAIK STORIES"
THE MONSTER WAS A GHOUL

☞ THE FOLLOWING was published in the *Athens Banner Watchman* on February 19, 1884:

FEEDING UPON GRAVES.

The strange animal which has been desecrating graves in Perry Township, Wood county, has again been seen. A gentleman whose veracity is not questioned gives this description of the novel grave-yard ghoul: Its neck and breast are white and the rest of the body is black; the tracks of its front feet are about eight inches long and three wide, making impressions in the snow with its claws about twice the length of a man's finger. The tracks made by the hind feet are nearly round, and about the size of a large dog's, except the claws, which are longer and sharper. The animal is about, three feet long and eighteen inches high.

It burrows into the ground in the grave yard, and penetrating the coffins therein contained; devours the contents thereof. It travels with such rapidity that all attempts thus far to kill it have been futile. The man who last saw the animal says it was in the middle of the road, having gone from a farm by literally tearing the fence to pieces. His dog gave chase to the animal, but soon returned scared almost to death.

The people living, in the vicinity having frequently heard loud noise which are supposed to have emanated from this peculiar unnamed, unknown beast. The animal is said to be slowly working its way to Toledo.

This animal sounds a bit like the Wahhoo covered in the previous chapter, as it too dug up graves to get at the corpses, so perhaps it was?

17
VALLEY OF THE WHISTLING WHATSITS
ISCHYROMYS ALIVE?

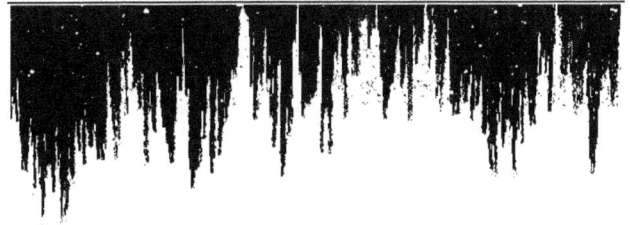

I DIDN'T QUITE KNOW what to make of this article, or whether or not it was even worth including. But, the men involved do seem to be describing heretofore unknown creatures, the likes of which are not reported on today. As always, the possibility remains that the men were witness to a remnant population of Ice Age survivors, in this case, prehistoric rodents.

The story was reported in the *Yazoo Sentinel* on September 10, 1891:

Strange Creatures That Infest the Olympic Mountains.

The Whatcom (Wash.) Reveille has the following: After lunch we passed through a beautiful piece of bottom land, teeming with flowers, red and yellow monthly musk, fringing the banks of the stream where it spread out over the meadow in a dozen different channels. Charlie wanted to stop and take up 100 acres, but Campbell told him, "Too much plenty snow in winter," and after vainly trying to drink the creek dry, we passed on. Another turn brought us to the base of a steep, bare, stony mountain. Skirting this and climbing over some big rocks we suddenly came into a lovely grass country. Like the prairie in summer, every conceivable flower seemed to bloom and blossom in the grass; the place was ablaze with red, blue, yellow and white.

We must have passed through 500 or 600 acres of it, and every here and there a rippling stream ran wildly through it. The place was a perfect paradise, and, thank goodness, we had got out of the dark valley and stood in the bright, warm sunshine. We were now close to the head of the Quileene, and we eagerly pressed on. Presently we met a dog, and close after him his master, who turned out to be Mr. Ransom, going from the head of the Dungeness of Port Townsend. He gave us cheerful accounts of the elk and also kindly took a letter into town for us. At 5:30 o'clock we camped under Sentinel rock, about a mile from the divide. This rock stands boldly out alone, like a massive fortress, guarding the entrance to the valley of the Dungeness.

Suddenly the mountain sides seemed to be alive with men whistling to one another, when - and one would turn sharp around only to hear another and a shriller whew - on the other side; and soon we saw lots of animals; about the size of a fox, with long, bushy tails, running about from rock to rock, sometimes lying down, but more often sitting bolt up, erect, as a ferret does. We shot a couple of small ones that night, and afterwards shot several more larger ones. Campbell called them whistling dogs, and declared they were good to eat but the smell was enough for us. Their odor is peculiar, but not fragrant. They have two long teeth in front like a beaver, and feet almost shaped like a squirrel's feet. I believe their right name is mountain beaver.

Wherever we went afterwards in the mountains, as long as there was grass, we saw these whistling dogs, as we got to call them. I liked to see them; they seemed to make the place cheerful and lively and were very amusing to watch. In winter they have long burrows under the snow, and their coats get a dark grey; in summer they are yellow. Their skins should make a good fur, and I think would pay for being trapped in the winter months. Our altitude this night was 5,450 feet, and we christened the place "Stone Camp," from the terribly stony ground we had to sleep on. The night was warm until about 4 o'clock a.m. when it got fearfully cold, and we were almost frozen.

Upon reading this story, I scoured prehistoric reference books for animals that might match the descriptions of the witnesses, the most important aspects being the prominent two front teeth, the bodily proportions of a fox, and feet and a bushy tail like that of a squirrel's. The closest match I could find was the prehistoric rodent, the Ischyromys. The animal was about two feet long (pretty close to a fox), with a squirrel-like bushy tail and feet. It also had prominent front incisors.

If nothing else, this encounter shows that cryptids are not always terrifying monsters, and can occasionally be cute, cuddly, and—according to this article—tasty.

Sources:

Benedict, Adam. *Monsters in Print: A Collection Of Curious Creatures Known Mostly From Newspapers.* Janesville: WI, 2019.

Cox, Barry and Colin Harrison. *The Simon & Schuster Encyclopedia of Dinosaurs & Prehistoric Creatures.* New York: Simon & Schuster, 1999.

18
SPRING CREEK CAVEMAN
BLUE MAN OF THE OZARKS

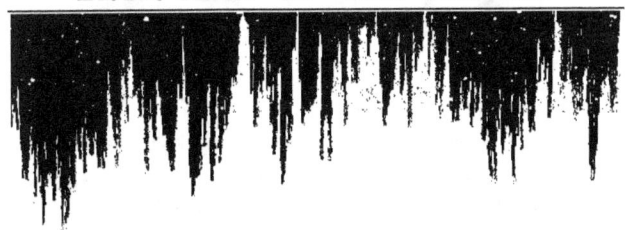

EARLIER IN THIS BOOK, I recounted a story about what seemed to be a modern-day man who had reverted back to the lifestyle of his stone-age ancestors. The "caveman" from this chapter, however, looks to be a different sort altogether. The sighting took place in the early months of 1865, in Spring Creek, Missouri. The source I'm using is a reprint that appeared in the *Caruthersville Democrat Argus* on December 2, 1924:

"Blue Man of Spring Creek", Strange Legend of the Ozark Mountains

The story of "The Blue Man of Spring Creek," has been current in the rough region in the eastern part of Douglas County, Mo., for 60 years. It is a genuine Ozark legend, and, if the testimony of scores of men during all these years is to be accepted, the legend is absolutely true.

It was in the winter of 1865 that a noted hunter of that part of the Ozarks, by the name of Sol. Collins,[41] was on the ridge that forms the watershed between the Big North Fork and Spring Creek. There was snow on the ground and Collins was utilizing it to trail the game, with which the hills abounded. Suddenly among the many tracks with which he was familiar, he came upon one such as he had never seen before. There were bears in the Ozarks in those days, and the hunter had trailed and slain many a one of them, in his time. This track looked somewhat like that of a bear, but if it was made by a bear then certainly here was the largest of the tribe that ever roamed the Ozark hills. In the deep snow the great foot prints were longer and broader than those of any bear Collins had ever seen, and at each side of the tracks were marks in the snow such as might have been made by long claws.

The hunter at once took up the trail, determined to kill the biggest bear in Ozark history. For hours he kept on tirelessly following those great foot prints. Far away to the north, almost to Indian Creek, then in a wide semicircle to the west, until he was close above the

---

[41] Sol Collins was a legendary figure himself, having fought in the War of 1812. He wanted to fight in the Civil War so badly that he had lied about his age to do so (he claimed he was in his forties when, in fact, he was in his seventies!).

ICE AGE

Big North fork. Still up hill and down the seemingly endless chase continued.

At last, as he was climbing the north slope of Upper Twin mountain, he heard a noise on the hillside above him, and looking up, was barely in time to leap to one side and allow a great boulder to sweep past him and crash into the depths of the valley. Another quickly followed the first, and Collins was glad to spring out of its path and shelter himself behind a big postoak. As he did so the third boulder struck fairly against the tree and was hurled with such force that it was shattered into fragments. The startled hunter ventured to peer cautiously from his shelter, to learn from whence this avalanche of boulders came. That which he saw fairly froze the blood in his veins, for there, on the hillside towered a gigantic figure shaped like an immense man, stark naked except for the skin of some animal around its waist and other wrappings around its feet. The creature was covered from head to foot with a tightly curling coat of short black hair, which as the sun struck upon it took on a dark blue hue. Collins always claimed that the giant was not less than nine feet tall, and his estimate is among the least of many made by other men in the years to follow.

Fled For His Life.

The hunter stared only long enough to make these observations before the creature cast aside the great ten foot club he carried, and tore out another boulder from the frozen ground, and hurled it with such deadly aim that again the tree was struck, and the rock shattered, and as he hurled the rock the giant lifted up his voice and made the hills echo and re-echo with an ear-splitting scream, more terrifying than ever came from any wild beast that roams the woods.

That was enough for Collins. He was no coward, and had creditably borne his part during the years of Civil war, but he never denied that after this one look, and that horrible scream, he took to his heels and fled for his life.

The hunter made it his business to gather several of his neighbors, sturdy hill men like himself, and for several days they put in most of their time following the tracks of the giant. Time and again they caught glimpses of him at a distance, going through the woods at a speed that at once left his pursuers far behind but no man was able to get within rifle shot of the creature. For two or three weeks the hunt continued almost every day, without result. The wild man was seen by numbers of people, and the occupants of more than one lonely cabin were awakened at dead of night by the most blood-curdling yells and shrieks in the dark woods, and when day dawned would find that sheep had been carried away, or a pig stolen from the pen. The hunters found bloody fragments of the animals thus carried off but the giant himself was never found.

After the first appearance of the "Blue Man," as he was now called, he disappeared for nine years. Then when most people who had not

ICE AGE

seen him had decided that the whole story was a fake, in the autumn of 1874 the word passed through the hills that the "Blue Man" had returned. Again were sheep and swine caught and devoured; again did men organize and hunt through the hills in a vain endeavor to capture or slay the creature, and again he escaped them all, and after creating a reign of terror for a week or two, disappeared as mysteriously as before.

Seen And Heard By Many.

During the next sixteen years he made two or three visits to the hills along the Big Fork. Always he was seen or heard by many, although he caught and devoured some of the smaller farm animals, but although hunted with greatest vigor he escaped unhurt as before. Evidently, however, the hunters had made it too hot for their strange quarry for this time he remained away for many years, and from 1890 to 1911 nothing was seen of him. New comers in the region ridiculed the fearsome tales told them by the old settlers and probably a majority of the inhabitants were of the belief that the story was the invention of some superstitious and scared hill man.

But suddenly he was again in the hills. Many unbeliever in his existence saw with their own eyes, that the old time story was undoubtedly true. More men than ever joined the hunt this time, and it was reported that they had discovered the creature's den in a cave in a remote valley, and that the floor of the place was strewn with the bones of the animals he had eaten, and his bed of dried leaves was seen in a corner. But again, as before, the mysterious creature disappeared.

In 1915 some loggers near Willow Springs claimed they saw the Blue Man at Blue Rock Mountain. And unlike some perennial cryptids that retain the same appearance, the Blue Man of the Ozarks even showed his age, as evidenced by this report from 1915:

> Jay Taber saw him less than a week ago. His hair, once black, is now gray and his body is not so robust as it was fifty years ago when Blue Sol Collins saw him first, but he is still very active and is probably the best living example of the simple life.

Interest in the Blue Man flared up again in 1925. Apparently, the postmaster in Ava, Missouri, had received questions about the Blue Man recently via a letter from California. The postmaster then decided to make up some tall tales for amusement, claiming in the *Nevada Daily News* in March 1925 that:

> "The clipping you enclosed is stated in facts," the postmaster wrote. "However, this man is now dead, but many of his children now live in a wild state on the banks of Spring creek, all colored blue, live in nude and subsist on small wild animals such as bear, wild cats and

ICE AGE

mountain lion, which these people devour raw. Many of them are 7 to 8 feet tall and weigh 300 to 500 pounds and are often seen carrying young horses and cattle on their shoulders to their dens or large caves where they live."

Though amusing, jokes like these hurt the credibility of the real stories, which seemed to have actually occurred. Overall, the earlier accounts had some similarities to a Sasquatch sighting in that the being was profusely hairy. Sasquatch also have been noted to throw rocks in the past.

An expedition has been organized to search for the "Blue Man of the Ozarks."

CARTOON FROM THE MID-1960s DEPICTING THE BLUE MAN AS A CAVEMAN.

NEANDERTHALS BY CHARLES KNIGHT C. 1920.

However, what sets this being apart from Bigfoot was its wearing of a loincloth, moccasins, and using tools—in this case, a stereotypical "caveman's club." Sasquatch are generally unclothed,[42] nor do they wear moccasins. As such, this sighting has more in common with a remnant Neanderthal than it does a Sasquatch—except for one thing. Neanderthals weren't all that tall, and the Blue Man was described as something of a giant.

And yet, the Blue Man of the Ozarks isn't the only anomalous cryptid of its kind. A similar being terrorized the Kentucky River hills in March of 1907. It was described as a "hair covered man thing" and wore a coonskin loin cloth.

As with the Blue Man, we don't know if it was a Sasquatch, a hairy wildman, a remnant Neanderthal, or something else entirely.

---

[42] In the interest of being thorough and objective, yes, Sasquatch are sometimes spotted wearing primitive garments, but this is very rare!

19

HIDEOUS MAN-EATER

ANOTHER WHATSIT

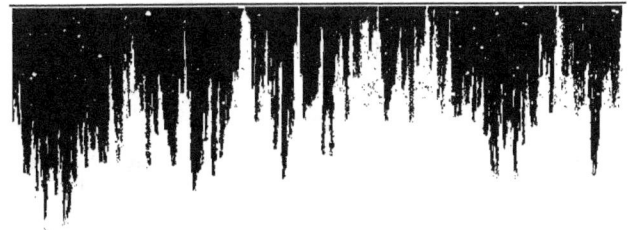

WHAT WE HAVE HERE is another of those maddening accounts where everyone gives either a vague description of the cryptid or an account that contradicts the last somewhat. As usual, it's nearly impossible to decide what kind of animal it may have been. But, whatever it was, it was indeed a monster...

From the *Neihart Herald* on June 22, 1895:

HIDEOUS MAN-EATER.
Montana
Along the Classic Banks of the Teton the Monster Frolics.

COWBOYS & SAURIANS

From time to time vague rumors have reached Great Falls of the depredations of a horrible monster which is reported to be roaming at large in Choteau county. Such fear has seized the people along Teton river that they have made every preparation against the monster, be it man or beast. Women and children are reported to have been frightened by the strange creature to such an extent that they have become seriously ill. Antelope and coyote hunters claim to have seen it skulking along the brush along the Teton, and ranchers claim that at night, hearing disturbances in the sheep pens, they have hastened forth, but just in time to see the brute escaping with a choice mutton wether clutched in his strange talons.

Many scoff at the stories circulated and profess to believe that the animal is a wolf of great size and unusual courage, but others, more credulous, claim that the animal has avoided bait which would tempt any wolf and say that it is invulnerable to bullets from any ordinary rifle.

One rancher claims that recently, while his wife was returning from the hen house, about noon, she heard a commotion among the poultry, and returning to the hen house to investigate, as she opened the door a monstrous beast leaped over her head, its hot breath being plainly felt upon her face, and with a sound like a human moan, it disappeared around a building before she had recovered from her fright. A lady who was riding along a trail recently saw a queer beast loping along ahead of

ICE AGE

her and gave chase to it. She had nearly overtaken it, when it turned and with a cry, more of agony than of terror, rushed past her, frightening her horse so that he threw his rider.

The Ford Benton River Press says of the beast: "Morgan Williams, who came in from the Teton today, reports there was great excitement in his neighborhood yesterday. A sheep shearer came in on horseback at a breakneck speed, dashing through wire fences and other obstacles, and explained his hurry by declaring that he had been chased over the prairie by a hideous man-eating monster. From the description given of the animal it appeared to be a cross between a mountain lion and a buffalo, its size comparing with that of a 2-year old heifer."

Others declare that the animal is nearer the size of a Norman stallion, with the agility of a monkey and the grace of a panther. It is said to have the voice of a human being, but no one has been able to get an accurate description of it.

Initially, this article threw me a bit when the writer made the comment "be it man or beast." Naturally, from that remark, I thought the story might have involved a Sasquatch, but that is clearly not the case. If anything, this story would sound like a routine ABC (alien big cat) if not for its great size. To combine some of the witness's descriptions, they were describing something that looked like "a cross between a mountain lion and a buffalo" that was the size of "a Norman stallion."

COWBOYS & SAURIANS

Though a feline would seem to be the top candidate due to its movements, most of the prehistoric felines weren't anywhere near the size of a horse. Therefore, once again, our friend the Sarkastodon would seem to be the most likely match in terms of size and description (though I can hardly imagine it moving "with the grace of a panther"). And, considering multiple witnesses claimed it gave off noises like a human, I'm almost tempted to draw parallels to the Shunka Warak'in, also said to emit cries like a human being at times. However, the creature described here was much too large to match up with the Shunka Warak'in.

Without any further details, this animal will have to remain classified as yet another "Whatsit" in a long line of strange creatures sighted in the late 1800s.

"SNAIK STORIES"
PREHISTORIC HYENA

THE *DAILY ADVOCATE* published a story on what could be a prehistoric hyena called the Percocruta on May 20, 1910:

Killed Strange Animal.

Church Point, La., May.17.— Upon making the rounds of his stable yesterday morning, Newton Barousse found that his mule colt had been killed, and partly devoured, the colt's head and neck, left foreleg and part of the shoulder being eaten away. Allowing the carcass to remain unmolested, Mr. Barousse lay in wait the following evening with his shotgun, and was successful in killing a very strange looking animal that had evidently come to make a meal off of the remains of its victim. The animal's neck, shoulders and forelegs were unusually developed and about twice the proportion of the hindquarters, which were fully six inches lower than the front portion of the body. The ears were long and sharp and the tail only six inches in length and quite thick. A growth of hair on the neck was about three inches long. No decision has been reached as to its identity, although it strongly resembles both a wolf and a hyena.

TYRANNOSAURUS OF THE TUNDRA C.1915.

20
TYRANNOSAURUS OF THE TUNDRA
IMITATOR OR COUSIN OF THE KERATOSAURUS?

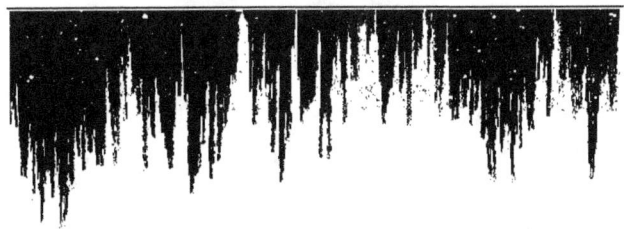

THE FOLLOWING fantastic story, in all likelihood, is just a copycat of the better known Ceratosaurus of the Arctic Circle stories, popular at the same time. This article even gives the Tyrannosaurs the kangaroo-like behavior that the Ceratosaurus also exhibited. And perhaps the final nail in the coffin is the fact that the writer at the time copyrighted his article—one typically copyrights works of fiction, not newspaper articles. The story was published in numerous papers across the country, but I found this particular version on page 15 of the *Ogden Daily Standard* published on April 15, 1916. My biggest nagging question about the story is, was it first published on April 1st?

COWBOYS & SAURIANS

Is the Deadly Dinosaur Dining Near the North Pole!

Folks up in Fairbanks, Alaska, who were accustomed to cold chills traversing their backs, got a series of unusually heavy ones the other day when a party of Eskimos came trekking into the town and told a story of a gigantic beast which they said, was living up near the North Pole.

The story might have been catalogued along with the regular list of Eskimo fairytales were it not for the fact that the description given of the monster tallies in every detail with that of the dinosaur, a huge creature of prehistoric times which scientists always contended passed off the face of the earth more than a million years ago.

But if the story of the Eskimos has any semblance of truth in it members of the dinosaur family are living in a strange northern land, believed to be the new continent discovered by Vilhjalmur Stefansson.[43] Furthermore, the section in which they are making their abode is warm, devoid of snow and gets its temperate conditions from hot water springs in the huge lake of steaming warm water.

---

[43] Stefansson was one of the great explorers of the Arctic, and was an advocate for the Northern regions and the peoples that lived there. He had hoped to find an entirely new continent in the region. While he never did find a whole continent, he did discover the following islands in the North Pole: Brock, Mackenzie King, Borden, Meighen, and Lougheed Islands.

ICE AGE

Sounds weird, doesn't it? But there are queerer things in Yellowstone National Park. Therefore, the story of the "warm country near the North Pole" and of the "big demons" said to be living in it cannot be branded as "impossible."

WAS KING OF BEASTS.

Among those who heard the tales of the Eskimos was Henry C. Coe, Junior, son of Henry C. Coe, a famous New York physician. The story soon found its way to New York and then to the American Museum of Natural History. Officials of that great institution declared, after hearing of the "northern monster," that the description fitted in every detail that of the Tyrannosaurus, a gigantic flesh eating reptile of the Cretaceous age, who in his time was the "king of peace."

The Tyrannosaurus was a member of the dinosaur family. A skeleton of one just has been mounted in the American Museum. It is 48 feet in length and 18 feet high. Also it has a head like a barrel, and double rows of long, sharp teeth. While officials of the American Museum express themselves as being more than doubtful as to the truth of the story told by the Eskimos, they still, figuratively speaking, "held an ace in the hole" by quoting from "Hamlet":

"There are more things in heaven and earth, Horatio, than their philosophy ever dreamed of."

COWBOYS & SAURIANS

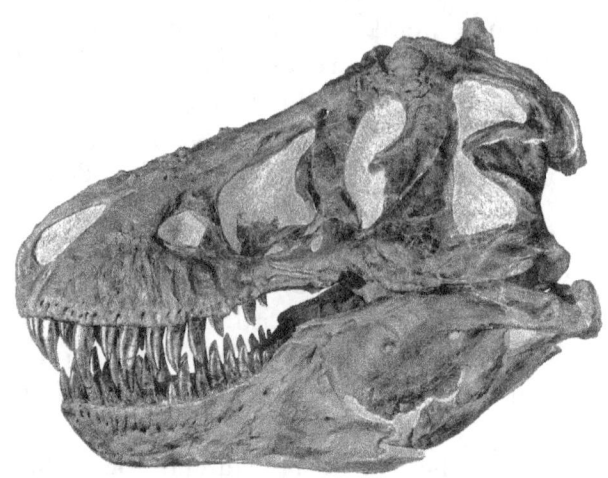

TYRANNOSAURUS SKULL C.1911.

Now for the tale of the Eskimos. Several weeks ago a straggling band of them trailed into Fairbanks. A grizzled old man led them. He carried a piece of frozen flesh about a foot square. His band had skins to trade, and one of the white men who was dickering with them asked what they intended doing with the piece of frozen flesh. The old man drew back in apparent alarm.

"Him great luck-giver," he said. "We no sell him"

"No flesh, no bird that flies, no anything, Him comes from big demon. Big demon kill two of our tribe. Him bring great luck."

ICE AGE

SWEPT TO A STRANGE LAND.

It was with difficulty and much patience that the trader got from the Eskimos the story of the frozen piece of flesh, which was the story of the "big demon."

The Eskimo said that more than a year ago he and about 50 others were living on Thetis island, off the northern extremity of Alaska. One day his son and 11 other men of the tribe went on a fishing expedition which carried them over the ice of the Arctic Ocean. There was a sudden breaking up of the ice, one of those catastrophes of the far north which are the dread of every Arctic explorer.

On a huge floe the 12 Eskimos were carried out to sea. They had a few fish with them. They also had a fire making machine, but very little else. They devoured the fish raw and remained huddled together on the floe, fearful lest it should split up again and hurl them into the icy water. For many days they drifted in the Arctic Ocean. The days stretched out into weeks, and the little band had given itself up for lost. But far-off through the northern mist land was sighted. The flow drifted in that direction.

The Eskimos saw not only land, but mountain ranges – a strange, new country to them. Making their way ashore they found signs of gaming – of the musk ox, the Arctic Fox and reindeer. Having their own primitive weapons with them, they managed to get food enough to keep them alive, and at the same time wandered inland, hoping to find human beings.

For many days, they said, they tracked through the mountainous country. Finally they reached the top of a particularly high ridge and there surveyed their surroundings. To their great joy they saw far off in the distance a land which to them appeared to have fertility in it. They began the journey toward it.

But when they reached the bottom of the ridge the land was no longer in sight. Another observation showed the seemingly fertile country was on a plateau, which made it invisible from the base of the mountains. So they journeyed toward the plateau. To their amazement, the snow became softer and finally disappeared entirely as they neared it.

The high, flatland was reached by a long, narrow pass, through which ran a stream of warm water! The temperature of the water aroused the superstitions of the Eskimo band, but they were desperate and continued ahead. When they reached the plateau they found it to be marshy land. In the middle of it was a large lake, from which clouds of steam were issuing.

Game abounded on the water heated land. The Eskimos obtained food enough for a fine repast and then had their first comfortable sleep since they had been carried away from Thetis Island. After many hours their leader was aroused by peculiar whining noises. He peered over a rocky formation on which they had been sleeping and there, according to the story he told his father, and which the father repeated in Fairbanks, he saw a monster fully 50 feet in length, with a huge head, a long neck and a long tail. Its hind legs were large and powerful; its forward ones were short.

FIND BOILING LAKE

Now, the Eskimo never had seen a kangaroo, but his description of the Arctic demon fitted that of a kangaroo, except in the respective sizes of the two creatures.

The panic stricken Eskimo aroused a companion and pointed toward the beast.

"The gods may have cursed us," said the companion. "They led us to a warm place with plenty of food and then they made our minds work the wrong way. We are seeing what is not, my brother."

This is according to the tale of the old Eskimo. The two men then aroused the other members of their party. All agreed that some 200 yards from them there flopped about in the marshy land a tremendous beast, which paused now and then to utter a peculiar wining sound – the noise that had attracted the attention of the Eskimo leader.

Being superstitious in the extreme, the Eskimos decided finally that the God of fortune had blessed them with comfort and then cursed them with false vision. To propitiate the god they told two of their number to approach the monster and speak to it in the hope that it would vanish. The two young Eskimos started off reluctantly.

COWBOYS & SAURIANS

OUTDATED RECONSTRUCTION OF TYRANNOSAURUS BY CHARLES KNIGHT C.1919.

ICE AGE

As they advanced toward the "demon" it turned, eyed them for only a few moments and charged. The men easily dodged it, whereupon it turned, made a second charge, gave its tail a tremendous alligator-like twitch and felled the Eskimos. Then it deliberately hopped up to the prostrate and unconscious pair and devoured them.

PLATEAU A GRAVEYARD

All of the remaining Eskimos still believe that they were laboring under some sort of spell, that the monster was not real, that their companions had not been killed but would be restored to them by their "god of fate" as soon as they left the land of the hot water. So they crawled down from their rock eminence and crept away from the plateau. But in the snowy wastes food became scarce and finally they were compelled by hunger to return.

This time the "demon" was not in sight. The Eskimos killed what game they wanted and stocked up with plenty of food. Some of it they "cached" on the rock stretch on which they had slept. Then they proceeded to explore the plateau. It seemed to be an "animal graveyard". Bones lay on all sides. Evidently the "demon" had more of its kind, for in every direction were huge three-toed marks which could have been made by nothing but a monster of the species that had devoured the two men.

During one of the hunts by the Eskimos they came upon the dead body of a "demon." From it they cut a huge section of skin and flesh, to take with them as proof of their astounding experience. Then, over near the edge of the hot water lake, they saw a live "demon" pursuing a musk ox. It ran with a motion which the Eskimos described as a "tumbling rush." Without difficulty it overtook the panic stricken musk ox as it had done with the two men.

The sight was too much for the little Eskimo band. They had seen enough. They voted to go back to the land of snow and ice and take no chances in the "domain of the demon."

So with the food they had "cached" they made their way off the fertile plateau, put back into the snowy mountains, wandered till the midnight sun disappeared and finally reached the ocean. There, footsore and heartsick, they put themselves on an ice flow and prayed to the "god of fate" to blow them back to their land. After many weeks they reached it and returned to Thetis Island where they told their wonderful story. Then, to silence all doubters, they produced the piece of hide and flesh which had been taken from the dead "demon."

"And so we make him demon and the good luck giver for tribe, and it bring plenty of luck," concluded the old Eskimo who told the story in Fairbanks.

ICE AGE

Now, what do scientists say of it all? Dr. W.D. Matthews[44] of the American Museum of Natural History made this declaration:

DR. WILLIAM DILLER MATTHEW.

"There is no possibility of the race of dinosaurs or any other creatures of that existing on earth today. There may be parts of the earth where the mammoth or the mastodon could exist, but not so the great dinosaurs."

Asked concerning the characteristics of the beast, and especially the Tyrannosaurus, his

---

[44] I'm actually quite surprised that Dr. William Diller Matthew, a respected paleontologist that worked at the American Museum of Natural History, took the time to even consult on the wild story. Matthew started out at the American Museum of Natural History as Assistant Paleontologist but had promoted to become the Curator in Chief of the Earth Sciences in 1922.

remarks sounded remarkably like the description given by the Eskimo.

"It was the largest of flesh eating monsters of the Cretaceous, which means that it lived 3 or 4 million years ago," said Dr. Matthew. "And it preyed on all living things, even the other dinosaurs, whether flesh eating or vegetarians."

Concerning its fighting qualities and methods he said:

HAD LITTLE INTELLIGENCE
"Their battles were mighty, and a fight between two of the Tyrannosaurus type must have been a fearsome spectacle. The evidences are that the fight was usually over some conquered and fallen animal. Our specimen, which is the only one mounted, is 47 ½ feet long, 18 ½ feet high, as posed, and I may say the pose was selected for the mounting after a very careful study of the way the bones ought to be put together and the animals habits as we know them.

"This skeleton," continued the doctor, "came from Hell Creek Beds, Montana, and it is known that all that part of the country was in the time that these monsters lived close to sea level, had a tropical climate and was covered with tropical vegetation there were huge animals of the vegetarian type even larger than the Tyrannosaurus for them to pray on, but no match for them in strength or ferocity.

"None of them had much intelligence and it is probable the method of fighting of the

ICE AGE

Tyrannosaurus was to make a wild rush, hit or miss, and grab what it encountered."

This is certainly the fashion of attack told about by the Eskimo, but Dr. Matthew smiled when reminded of it. At any rate, the story of the "the great demon" is being told in all the igloos of northern Alaska these days, and Eskimo mothers are saying to their youngsters who insist on going out when the ice isn't any too solid in the Arctic Ocean:

"Be careful, oh, little child. The god of fate may frown, and then the wind will blow and you will be carried to the land of the great demon."

And straightaway the "boy" runs into the igloo, crying lustily for all the Eskimo children believe the "demon over the water" isn't a living thing, but a ghost, and can travel anywhere and any length of time. Selah!

I halfway wondered if such an obvious work of fiction should have even been included in this book. For instance, some of you may have noticed I did not include the story "The Killing of the Mammoth" printed in *McClure's Magazine* in 1899. It was identified as a work of fiction in the magazine's table of contents, and still readers believed that it was true! This story, however, I have found little to no discussion on in cryptozoology circles. Or, in other words, no one has come out to completely denounce it yet that I have seen.

COWBOYS & SAURIANS

Another reason I did include the story is that it ties into a prevalent myth about a warm oasis full of prehistoric creatures in the wilds of Alaska...

POSTSCRIPT
THE REAL LAND THAT TIME FORGOT
THE PREHISTORIC ALASKAN OASIS

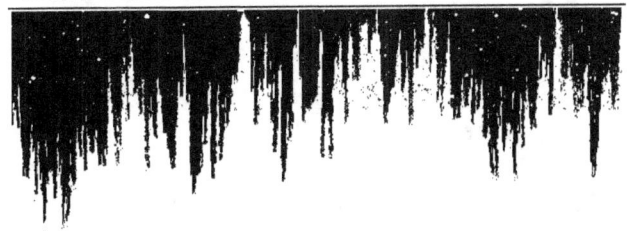

IN 1917 EDGAR RICE BURROUGHS published one of his more famous novels, *The Land That Time Forgot*. Like *The Lost World*, it told of a hidden land of prehistoric survivors, only Burroughs's version was hidden by walls of thick ice near Antarctica, on an island south of South America. To the North, in the Arctic regions, if newspaper reports are to be believed, there may be similar "Lands That Time Forgot" hidden away for real.

In the 1900s, trappers in the Alaskan wilderness told tales of a hidden tropical valley. They theorized these lands were heated by subterranean volcanic activity, which also produced lush vegetation. Occasionally these lands also contained tracks of huge monsters.

The first newspaper report of the lost valley came from the *Corvallis Times* on September 16, 1903:

MADE BIG TRACKS.
BELIEF THAT A MASTODON STILL SURVIVES IN ALASKAN VALLEY.

Its Track, Twenty Inches Long - Followed by Portland Man Until They Entered Cave and Disappeared.

Portland, Sept. 11. - The Portland Journal says: Dr. John P. Frizzell is organizing an expedition in Portland to bring back to this city the body of a mastodon which he firmly believes exists upon Unimak island, off the western coast of Alaska. Dr. Frizzell, while employed as a United States surgeon on that island, on July 4, 1903, saw tracks which were 20 inches long by 19 ½ wide, followed them for two miles inland, and traced the course of the monster into a cave that makes into the side of a volcano. Dr. Frizzell was accompanied by James Nugent, James Geary and S.F. Smith sailors from the Nellie Coleman, a San Francisco ship. These sailors corroborate Dr. Frizzell's statements. Geary himself measured the tracks, and all of the party agree regarding the evidences of the presence there of an animal the like of which has never been known to naturalists as living in the modern times. So tangible are these evidences that

ICE AGE

prominent citizens of Portland propose to back him in an expedition to hunt and kill that mastodon.

When Dr. Frizzell and the three sailors discovered the track, they had gone in the ship's dory 16 miles to the north end of the island. They were on a caribou hunt, and seven miles inland toward Sheshalda mountain[45] and Pomgronni mountain, in a valley between the two, the doctor saw the imprints in the earth, to which he called the attention of his companions.

"Up there on Unimak island, where I was stationed as surgeon for the government," said Dr. Frizzell yesterday, "is a region so fascinating that I propose to return. I have hunted in New Zealand, Van Dieman's land, Mexico, Florida, Canada, and in other countries. My father was one of the famous rifle shots of Ireland. I have hunted since I was 8 years old. Yet I know of no country in which are such marvels as are found in the Far North within the limits of the United States possessions.

"When we found those enormous tracks, they were several feet apart and looked as though one had made them with a stable bucket turned upside down on the earth. On the outer rim in front was the mark of what was apparently a horny substance, while inside were smaller marks as though of numerous toes running around the inside of the rim. The tracks are

---

[45] He means Mount Shishaldin, a moderately active volcano on Unimak Island.

larger than those of an elephant. We followed them for two miles and established the fact that the monster inhabited a cave in the side of a volcano. This volcano is active, emitting every five minutes smoke and ashes, which showed for two miles down the mountain side.

MT. SHISHALDIN BY C. NYE, ALASKA DIVISION OF GEOLOGICAL AND GEOPHYSICAL SURVEYS, C.1994.

"The valley of which I speak is between Mount Sheshalda, 9,500 feet high, and Pomgronni, 6,000 feet high. One the sides of these mountains grow luxuriantly beautiful specimens of the lupen, violets with stocks a foot long and blossoms two inches across, strawberries luscious and of immense size, and various flora. Even so early as June the flowers come out with wonderful brilliancy. The ground at that time of year is warm from the heat of the underground fires, which accounts for the marvelous early advancement of all blooming.

ICE AGE

The strawberries are found in tracts acres in extent.[46]

Tales of lush lands full of volcanoes and succulent produce would die away for a time, but there was a resurgence of such tales in the 1920s. The first from that era (that I can find) comes from the *Valdez Miner* from November 11, 1922. It told the tale of sea otter trapping duo Hank Russell and Jack Lee. While climbing a high arctic pass, the two spied a lush green valley below. From their high-top observation, it looked as though the land was settled in the dormant crater of a volcano. That this was the case became even more apparent when they descended down a narrow canyon and into the lost world. It was so hot there that they had to take off their parkas. Even that night when they made camp, the ground was so warm that they didn't need sleeping bags.

Many animals were observed across the lush landscape, which included a large lake and steaming fissures, but no dinosaurs or monsters. However, the two men did spy something else very interesting. The *Valdez Miner* recorded that:

In looking over the valley, the prospectors found tracks of several animal species unknown to them. These tracks were too large for bears, being some eighteen inches in diameter and perfectly round with three depressions in the front of the track resembling toes.

---

[46] Benedict, *Monsters in Print*, pp. 247-248.

COWBOYS & SAURIANS

Had they been living in a prehistoric age, the prospectors would have sworn the tracks to be those of mastodon or mammoth. A close search of the valley revealed no animal large enough to make tracks anywhere near this size, and unless the creature lived in the warm waters of the lake, they were unable to account for its whereabouts.

They also saw bear tracks of enormous size, and in places the bushes were torn up for several yards, branches being broken many feet from the ground.[47]

Unfortunately, Russell and Lee refused to tell anyone just where this valley was. We next see the valley mentioned in the July 25, 1924 *Alaska Weekly*. The article tells of a man named Captain Sam C. Scotte, who had a cabin in the lost world, here said to be located somewhere in the Liard River country in the Cassiar Mountains in British Columbia. He too talked of strange animals. *The Alaska Weekly* reported that:

Captain Scotte bears out the statement of Frank Perry, whom he knows and who is alleged to have discovered this strange land some years ago, as to the strange animals that inhabit this land. Scotte himself says he saw white deer there, a species that he never saw or heard of before, and that Casca John, an old Indian, told

---

[47] Ferrell, *Strange Stories of Alaska and the Yukon*, pp.57.

ICE AGE

him about animals very similar to musk oxen that inhabited the region.[48]

Next, "The Valley of Eden" was published in the June 26, 1925 issue of *Alaska Weekly*. It told of mining engineer Frank Perry, mentioned in the previous article, discovering the valley.

Crossing a range one winter and reaching the crest, Perry prepared to descend into the next valley when he was surprised to find the area covered with heavy fog. This valley was approximately 200 miles long and about 40 wide. Rivers of hot water ran through it, fed by hundreds of hot springs. These springs bubbled out of the ground, condensed, and formed a layer of fog.

Perry remained in the valley and its neighborhood for a year. Never before in his experiences had he seen so many wild animals which congregated there for the luxuriant vegetation made possible by the heat generated by the springs. In the valley were hundreds of mountain sheep, goats, caribou, and moose, with bears and other furbearing animals.

Due to the exceptionally good grazing in the valley, Perry stated that the moose and caribou looked like the pictures of the old Norman horse – almost square from fat – and they were so tame that he walked among them and could almost touch them as they fed.

---

[48] Ibid, pp.52.

THE GARDEN OF EDEN BY THOMAS COLE C.1828.

ICE AGE

This country was never visited by the Indians because of imprints of huge three toed prehistoric animals found in the sandstones and the shells. Indians thought these monsters still roam the country and, although they knew it to be a hunter's paradise, they gave the valley a wide berth.[49]

On September 24, 1925, the *Wrangell Sentinel* published the article "Where the Waters Run Warm." It told of a prospector and his companions sojourning in the valley where they saw flowers of immense size and more odd animals.

Col. Williams said that among the other interesting things he saw in the North were a white moose, doubtless an albino, and also white bear similar to the Beacon Hill Park animal in Victoria.[50]

All in all, most of the stories line up rather nicely with corroborating details like the strange species of white moose, the giant three-toed footprints, and fertile land. Could this really have been a hidden "land that time forgot" where Mammoths, Tyrannosaurs, and "Keratosaurs" ran wild? In summary, I would have to say: the mammoths, probably. The "Keratosaurus," maybe. But the Tyrannosaurus? Definitely not!

---

[49] Ibid, pp.48-49.
[50] Ibid, pp.54.

Sources:

Benedict, Adam. *Monsters in Print: A Collection Of Curious Creatures Known Mostly From Newspapers.* Janesville: WI, 2019.

Ferrell, *Strange Stories of Alaska and the Yukon.* Fairbanks, AK: Epicenter Press, 1996.

ACKNOWLEDGMENTS

For this volume, I only have a handful of people whom I need to thank. Thank you to my dear friend A'Lora Norris, a tintype photographer, who helped me with the question of whether or not one could, in fact, photograph a "Keratosaurus" in the wilds of Alaska in 1907. Thank you, Adam Benedict, author of *Monsters in Print*, for answering the odd question here and there. And a big thank you to Justin Mullis, who gave my Partridge Creek Monster chapter some much-needed peer review! It's with great sadness that I deliver this last thank you, though. Christopher Martinez, I only had the pleasure of knowing you for one year, but what a great year it was. Thank you not only for the great covers, but also for all the great conversations we had, spitballing ideas for future books and covers that I'm sad that we won't get to work together on. Chris lost a valiant battle with cancer in 2020 while he was working on the cover for this book. Even though he didn't get the chance to finish it, it's still beautiful, and I wouldn't replace it for anything. Rest in peace, Chris.

ARTIST'S PENCILS

INDEX

Adams, John "Grizzly", 150
Alaska, 17, 21, 45-48, 52-57, 63-64, 68, 83, 109-118, 141, 145-146, 231-252
Alien Big Cats, 11, 227
Andrewsarchus, 172
Arizona, 105, 210
Bear Lake Monster, 68-74
Billy the Kid, 85, 88
Blue Man of the Ozarks, 217-224
Borhyaena, 188
Borophagus, 129, 193
Brazil, 92-93
Brushy Bill Roberts, 85, 88
Budge, William, 71
Buffalo Bill Cody, 85
Buttler, James Lewis, 17, 22-31, 37
Canada, 11, 65-68, 74, 115, 148, 247
Castoroides ohioensis, 65, 74
Ceratosaurus, 13, 15-64, 231
Chain Lake monster, 157-167
Chupacabra, 181
Coleman, Loren, 129-130, 183, 246
Collins, Sol, 218
Colorado, 89, 133-140
Cynodontia, 172

Desmostylus, 171
Diademodon, 172
Dog Eater, The, 175-192
Dollo, Lois, 59
Dupuy, George, 17-21, 31-49, 54-55, 60-61, 63
Elasmotherium, 135-138
Foster, Lance M., 125, 128
Fothergill, Charles, 67
Georgia, 102, 169, 172
glyptodont, 92-93
Heilig, Sterling, 20-21, 57-58
Henry the Younger, Alexander, 66
Hollywood, California, 88
Hutchins, Israel, 127
Hutchins, Ross, 127
Idaho, 80-85, 89, 128-131, 199, 201, 203
Idaho Museum of Natural History, 130
Ingram, David, 11
Ioway Indians, 126
Ischyromys, 216
Kentucky, 176-177, 189-191, 224
Kirby, Jack, 130
Laelaps, 58-59
Lavagneux, Father Pierre, 1, 17-18, 22, 25-29, 34-39, 49, 54-55

Leemore, Tom, 17, 22-24, 28-42, 45, 49-50, 54-55, 63
MacFarlane, Robert, 148
MacFarlane's Bear, 147-151
Madison Valley History Museum, 130
Maine, 157-159
mammoth, 9-11, 13, 65, 79, 101, 115, 118, 109-123, 139, 241, 249
Matthew, Dr. W.D., 241
Mexico, 14, 79-82, 85-86, 247
Minhocão, 92, 93
Missouri, 217, 222
Monster Quest, 149
Montana, 125-131, 199, 203-204, 210, 225, 242
Mullis, Justin, 59
Neanderthals, 95, 100, 224
Nebraska, 91
Nevada, 95-96, 193, 199-200, 210, 222
Obruchev, Vladimir, 57
Ohio River Monster, 75-78
Olympic Mountains, 213
Pearson, Barney "Idaho Bill", 59, 80-89
Percocruta, 229
ringdocus, 128, 131
Rocky Mountain Range, 11, 13

sabertooth tiger, 79-80, 84, 88-89
Sanderson, Ivan T., 86-87
Sarkastodon, 101-102, 105-106, 173, 228
Sasquatch, 100, 223-224
Shuker, Karl, 64, 74, 80, 83, 88, 93-94, 156
shunka warak'in, 124-131, 210
Siberia, 20, 46, 53-57, 109, 118
Sivatherium, 155-156
Skinner, Alanson, 125
Smithsonian National Museum of Natural History, 60
South America, 92-93, 245
Stefansson, Vilhjalmur, 232
Thompson, David, 11
Thylacoleo, 188
Tombstone Pterodactyl, 13, 61, 105
Tombstone, Arizona, 64, 87
Trails to Nature's Mysteries: The Life of a Working Naturalist, 127
tyrannosaurs, 230-243
Wahhoo, 193-212
Weatherly, David, 106-107, 193, 210
White Rhinoceros, 133

ABOUT THE AUTHOR

John LeMay was born and raised in Roswell, New Mexico, famous for its 1947 UFO crash. He is a historian who has written over a dozen books, most of them on Southwestern history such as *Tall Tales and Half Truths of Billy the Kid*. He is the co-author/co-creator of *The Real Cowboys and Aliens* series with Noe Torres. Like the *Cowboys & Saurians* series, *The Real Cowboys and Aliens* explores UFO sightings and alien encounters of the Pioneer Period. LeMay is also a past president of the Historical Society for Southeast New Mexico and has written for magazines such as *Cinema Retro, True West, G-Fan, Mad Scientist* and *Xenorama*.

ALSO AVAILABLE

Long before the first airplane took flight, when nothing but birds should have been in the skies, the early residents of the United States witnessed bizarre unidentified flying objects of all sizes, shapes, and descriptions. They encountered strange beings that clearly were not human, including "Men in Black" and possibly time travelers. They saw huge motherships, underwater UFOs, and other unexplained wonders. Some of America's most famous early historical figures, including Thomas Jefferson, Ben Franklin, and George Washington, shared an interest in UFOs and extraterrestrials. Contained within these pages is the "other" American History that you were never taught in school!

UFO expert Nick Pope says, "If you think the UFO mystery began in 1947 with flying saucers and the Roswell crash, think again. This fascinating, data-rich book explores a wealth of intriguing incidents that were formerly interpreted through the lens of folklore, but which could now lead to a fundamental reappraisal of the greatest mystery of the modern age. With the focus on the 19th century, this delightful tome shines a light on a slice of American history that shows truth really can be stranger than fiction."

Best-selling author Donald Schmitt says, "What Torres and LeMay have clearly defined in this suspenseful thriller tome, is that the UFO accounts portrayed throughout this exhaustively researched work, remain in a separate class.... Aside from a rare hot-air balloon or dirigible, there was nothing else in the air back then... or on the ground; the witnesses are clearly describing something which precedes the Wright Brothers technology.... The simple fact that such cases exist in an era where the sky above us was still pristine and H. G. Wells had yet to conquer the Earth with Martians should captivate us all...."

Ruben J. Uriarte of the Mutual UFO Network adds, "Before airplanes were invented, journalists and scientists of the 19th century recorded hundreds of sightings of unidentified aerial phenomena crisscrossing the skies of America. This amazing new book provides a startlingly detailed look at these early UFO cases, which tend to confirm that we are not alone!"

Cowboys & Saurians: Dinosaurs and Prehistoric Beasts as Seen by the Pioneers, written by John Le May, author of *The Real Cowboys & Aliens: UFO Encounters of the Old West,* and published in September of 2019, is a collection of accounts from the late 19th and early 20th century detailing encounters with seemingly impossible saurians.

LeMay provides a helpful introduction at the beginning of the book to those for whom the idea of remnant dinosaurs might be new, which can be skipped by experienced cryptozoologists already familiar with the subject, before launching directly into the tales of Old West-era monsters with 'The Pterodactyl of Tombstone.' New fans and experienced researchers alike will appreciate his approach to the topic, as LeMay provides a nuanced, well-researched history of the controversial story and its associated photograph—which may or may not exist.

This author isn't afraid to delve into high strangeness, either, and if there are elements thereof existent in an account, LeMay will tell you about them. From the Piasa Bird to the Van Meter Visitor to the Marfa Lights, LeMay offers a wide array of phenomena from off the beaten path. He provides a plethora of sources for each, drawing from historical newspaper accounts and the previous explorations of his fellow cryptozoologists; even peppering the book with the original art and illustrations that went to print, whenever possible.

LeMay doesn't offer a lot of definitive solutions to the mysteries presented in this book, being content to provide the reader with the tools to make their own determination. These stories are wildly entertaining, but hard facts, let alone proof, are difficult to come by, and LeMay is well aware of the struggle intrinsic to the field. To that end, there's no agenda here; he's not trying to sell you a paradigm. The only bill of goods within this book is a batch of intriguing stories, retold with excellent research.

Cowboys & Saurians is a well-researched, open-minded tour of the Old West's most fantastic tales of saurian encounters; sure to appeal to both new seekers and established cryptozoological researchers alike.—Tobias Wayland, The Singular Fortean Society.

SPECIAL PREVIEW
SOUTHERNERS & SAURIANS
Swamp Monsters, Lizard Men, and Other Curious Creatures of the Old South

"An Uncanny Monster"

The people residing along Palmetto Creek [South Carolina]... as well as those for miles back in the slashes,' are highly excited over the appearance of a strange and uncouth creature in that vicinity. The beast is described as being a creature that far outdoes the nightmare ideas of the mythologists. It is equally at home in the water, on the land or among the tall trees of the neighborhood, where it has been most frequently seen. The general contour of the head reminds one of a gigantic serpent with this exception: The 'snout' terminates in a bulbus [sic], monkey faced knot, which much resembles the physiognomy of some gigantic ape. From the neck down, with the exception of some fin shaped flippers, which extend from the arms to the waist, the creature resembles a man, only that the toes and fingers are armed with claws from two to six inches long.

Tracks made by the beast in the soft mud around Hennis lake have been taken to Donners Grove, where they are kept on exhibition in a druggists showcase. Those who have seen the horn'd thing face to face say that it is a full nine feet in height, which could hardly be believed only for the fact that the tracks mentioned above are within a small fraction of fifteen inches in length. Fishermen who surprised the monster sitting silently on a mass of driftwood declared that its back looked like an alligator's, and that it had a caudal termination a yard long, which forked like the tail of a fish.

www.ingramcontent.com/pod-product-compliance
Lightning Source LLC
Chambersburg PA
CBHW071337080526
44587CB00017B/2866